Acknowledgements

Our sincere thanks to all those who contributed to the successful publication of this book. Laura would particularly like to thank her family, Terry, Alison and Dan, for their endless support and advice, with special thanks to Dan (her star) for his proofreading, first-class political knowledge and endless cups of tea. Robbi would like to give special thanks to her husband Erden, whose determination to join her in the UK led her to research the tortuous road of immigration law – and to explore the intricacies of the 'Life in the UK' test. With a lot of work, and a little help from Robbi, Erden passed the test first time and is now a UK resident. Thanks also to Carol Callegari, whose advice put them both on the right track to a successful visa application.

Further thanks are also due to Peter Read (editing & proofreading), Di Tolland (design and desktop publishing) and Jim Watson for the illustrations, maps and cover design. Finally, a special thank you to the many photographers (listed on page 222), whose images help bring the book to life.

What readers & reviewers have said about Survival Books:

'The ultimate reference book. Every subject imaginable is exhaustively explained in simple terms. An excellent introduction to fully enjoy all that this fine country has to offer and save time and money in the process.'

American Club of Zurich

'The amount of information covered is not short of incredible. I thought I knew enough about my birth country. This book has proved me wrong. Don't go to France without it. Big mistake if you do. Absolutely priceless!'

Reader

'When you buy a model plane for your child, a video recorder, or some new computer gizmo, you get with it a leaflet or booklet pleading 'Read Me First', or bearing large friendly letters or bold type saying 'IMPORTANT - follow the instructions carefully'. This book should be similarly supplied to all those entering France with anything more durable than a 5-day return ticket. – It is worth reading even if you are just visiting briefly, or if you have lived here for years and feel totally knowledgeable and secure. But if you need to find out how France works then it is indispensable. Native French people probably have a less thorough understanding of how their country functions. – Where it is most essential, the book is most up to the minute.

Living France

A comprehensive guide to all things French, written in a highly readable and amusing style, for anyone planning to live, work or retire in France.

The Times

Covers every conceivable question that might be asked concerning everyday life – I know of no other book that could take the place of this one.

France in Print

A concise, thorough account of the Do's and DONT's for a foreigner in Switzerland – Crammed with useful information and lightened with humorous quips which make the facts more readable.

American Citizens Abroad

'I found this a wonderful book crammed with facts and figures, with a straightforward approach to the problems and pitfalls you are likely to encounter. The whole laced with humour and a thorough understanding of what's involved. Gets my vote!'

Reader

Important Note

The UK is a diverse country with many faces and a multitude of nationalities, ethnic groups, religions and customs, added to which the UK has continuously changing laws, rules, regulations and prices. Always check with an official and reliable source (not always the same) before making any major decisions or taking an irreversible course of action.

Contents

The Authors

Laura Barnhouse

Laura is an experienced writer and journalist living with her fiancé in Bath. She has written for numerous magazines and newspapers, including *The Big Issue*, *Real Travel* and *The Birmingham Independent*, and is currently working on her first novel. As an avid traveller, she has first-hand experience of how baffling life in an alien environment can be, and trusts that readers will find this book invaluable and enjoy their new life in the UK.

Robbi Forrester-Atilgan

Robbi was born in the UK and has worked as a journalist for many years. She spent her early career working in the music press, travelling the world with rock acts such as Ozzy Osbourne and Bon Jovi, before settling for the more sedate world of freelance editing. As well as writing for a living, Robbi has worked as an airport representative, English teacher and estate agent.

Robbi first visited Turkey in the mid-'90s, where she met her future husband, and became a Turkish citizen through marriage in 2001. Her efforts to help her husband Erden to qualify for UK residency make her uniquely qualified to co-author this book. She and Erden now divide their time between the UK and their Turkish home in Dalyan, a small riverside town near the Mediterranean coast (no prizes for guessing which place they love most!). Robbi is also the author of *Culture Wise Turkey* (to be published by Survival Books in 2009).

Fermanagh, N. Ireland

Introduction

The United Kingdom is one of the most popular destinations in the world, particularly for those seeking a new life. Every year, thousands of people apply for a visa to visit the UK, and many more plan on staying for good. However, while Britain has a history of welcoming newcomers and has developed into a truly multicultural society – London is officially the most multicultural city in the world – it's also a small country with a growing number of social problems. There isn't room to accommodate every would-be resident, and therefore the British government has raised the bar by applying a test of its national language and culture, known as the 'Knowledge of Life in the UK' test.

The government has decided that in order to live without restriction in the UK, foreigners must acquire a certain level of knowledge about the country and competence in its language – which obviously makes good sense. You will struggle in Britain if you lack the English skills to go shopping, use public transport and complete official forms – and you will feel much more at home if you can understand the language. You will also feel more at ease around British people if you understand how their country works – and why.

The 'Life in the UK' test was first introduced as part of the citizenship process. But now, anyone wishing to become a permanent resident of the UK – and obtain a settlement stamp in their passport – must take and pass the test at an official test centre. It only takes around 45 minutes but those minutes can make or break your chance of settling in Britain.

Not surprisingly, an entire industry of guidebooks, websites and courses has grown up around the 'Life in the UK' test, but there's only one thing that will get you through it: a thorough knowledge of five chapters in the Home Office's *Life in the United Kingdom: A Journey to Citizenship* handbook. Absorbing that information is the key to a successful outcome.

The *Life in the UK: Test & Study Guide* has been written to help you make sense of the Home Office handbook. The information is clear and concise, with easy-to-grasp facts, simply explained. What's more, the authors know what they're talking about – Robbi coached her husband so well that he passed the test first time and is now settled into his new life in the UK. Here's hoping that you will do the same – and that this book will help you enjoy the journey.

Good Luck!

Laura Barnhouse & Robbi Forrester Atilgan

October 2008

Polperro, Cornwall

1.

INTRODUCING THE 'LIFE IN THE UK' TEST

So, you want to live in the UK – or you wouldn't be reading this book. You've heard about the 'Life in the UK' test, but maybe you're not sure what it is or how to go about taking and, more important, passing it. It could be that you've already looked at other books on the subject, but found them difficult to read or confusing.

We don't claim that the Life in the UK: Test & Study Guide can get you through the test without some hard work on your behalf, but its aim is to make the learning process more enjoyable, interesting and – ultimately – successful.

WHAT IS THE 'LIFE IN THE UK' TEST?

It's a short test designed to check whether, as a would-be UK resident or citizen, you can fit in with the British way of life. It does this by:

♦ testing your knowledge of the English language;

♦ testing your knowledge of British customs and institutions and other important aspects of living in the UK.

The test's full title is the 'Knowledge of Life in the UK' test, but it's generally referred to as the 'Life in the UK' test, which is what we call it in this book. It's based on chapters two, three, four, five and six of the Home Office's *Life in the United Kingdom: A Journey to Citizenship* handbook, and it's these chapters that are covered here.

The 'Life in the UK' test has a number of different names, which can be confusing. When it was first introduced in 2005, people called it the 'citizenship test', because it was taken by residents who wanted to become citizens of the UK. As it was a test for people aiming to become British, some also referred to it as the 'Britishness test'. However, everything changed in 2007, when the government decided that immigrants who wanted to become permanent residents first had to pass the 'Life in the UK' test.

Therefore, anyone applying for permanent residency or settlement status since 2nd April 2007 must take and pass the test. Even if you qualify for residency on all other counts, you cannot become a permanent resident of the UK until you have passed the test.

Both the *Life in the United Kingdom: A Journey to Citizenship* handbook and the test questions were revised in April 2007. This was done to make both more accessible and easier to understand for those whose mother tongue isn't English. The contents of the above book and the chapters that candidates need to learn have also changed. Make sure that your copy of the above book is the revised edition (see the cover) and that it's valid for tests taken after April 2007.

> Britain and the United Kingdom are two different names for the same country. Britain was once called Great Britain but has modestly dropped the 'Great'. The United Kingdom (UK) refers to the four countries which make up the nation – its full title is the United Kingdom of England, Scotland, Wales and Northern Ireland. Note that the southern part of Ireland is an entirely separate country.

WHY DOES BRITAIN NEED A 'LIFE IN THE UK' TEST?

Britain is a popular country with immigrants, and many people want to live there; figures from the UK Border Agency for 2006-7 show that 102,360 applications were made for settlement in this period, of which over 80 per cent were approved.

Britain is seen as a rich 'melting pot' of nationalities and languages. There are people from hundreds of different countries living in the UK, and you will hear numerous different languages. While it's celebrated for its diversity, the UK government – along with many British people – believes that anyone coming to live in Britain must make an effort to understand the country's culture and traditions, its laws and democracy and the way it's governed. They must also demonstrate an ability to speak its official language, English.

Together, the above skills enable new residents to feel comfortable, to work and fully integrate into British society, and to make a contribution to the community. The 'Life in the UK' test is a way of ensuring this.

Britain is not the only country to test would-be residents; Australia, Canada and the US all have similar tests for prospective residents.

HOW TO BECOME A UK RESIDENT

There's nothing to stop you living in Britain on a long-term basis by renewing and extending a temporary visa, but if you do this it's difficult to feel as if you really belong. Permanent residency is the next step and is often referred to as settlement, which means that you intend to settle in the UK on a permanent basis. The official term is 'indefinite leave to remain' (ILR) which is exactly what it says: you can stay in the UK for as long as you like, free from immigration control.

Most people must live in the UK for a period (a minimum of two years) before applying for indefinite leave to remain, which is known as the qualifying period. It varies according to your reasons for being in the UK, for example:

♦ you might be in Britain on a work permit ;

♦ you might be part of the highly skilled migrant programme;

♦ you might be someone with British ancestry, i.e. your grandparents were born in the UK;

♦ you might be a business owner;

♦ you might be a refugee claiming asylum (a place of safety);

♦ you might be the spouse (husband or wife) or civil partner or other relative of a UK national or resident;

♦ you might have been living in the UK for a long time.

You can apply for ILR after you've spent between 2 and 14 years living in Britain, depending on which of the above categories you qualify under. Spouses can apply after two years, while most other applicants must wait five years. People who've lived in the UK for ten years legally or those who entered the country illegally but have stayed for a minimum of 14 years, can also apply for ILR.

You cannot apply for ILR more than 28 days before the end of your qualifying period. If you do this, your application will be refused and you will lose your fee. In addition, you may be refused ILR if you've spent too much time outside the UK during this period unless you have a good reason, such as family illness or business travel.

You must meet other conditions in order to qualify for settlement, such as showing that you're employed or that you can support yourself and your dependents, or that you're in a genuine relationship. Just passing the 'Life in the UK' test isn't enough on its own.

Six Steps to Settlement

Step 1: Decide that you want to stay in the UK.

Step 2: Check your qualifying period and other requirements.

Step 3: Find out whether you need to take the 'Life in the UK' test.

Step 4: Study this book and take the test.

Step 5: Complete the form and apply for settlement.

Step 6: Settlement approved – you're now a UK resident.

The good news is that you only need take the test once. After you pass the 'Life in the UK' test and become a British resident, you can go on to apply for British citizenship at a later date without taking any more tests.

A study of 850,000 children in London schools revealed that they spoke over 300 different languages between them.

It's possible to take the 'Life in the UK' test while in Britain on a visitor's visa, prior to applying for settlement. This is especially useful for husbands, wives or civil partners of British citizens or residents. Provided you've lived with your partner for at least four years outside the UK, and can fulfil the other conditions for residency, and you pass the 'Life in the UK' test prior to applying for a spouse visa, you may be granted permanent residency straight away. You will, however, have to return to your country of origin to make the application.

Becoming a British Citizen

Citizenship is the next stage on from settlement and is usually obtained through a process known as naturalisation. It's optional – you don't have to become a British (UK) citizen. Many people are happy to remain as residents, and it's rare to lose the privilege unless you commit a serious crime or remain out of the UK for more than two years, in which case you may have to apply to come back as a returning resident. However, citizenship offers additional advantages:

◆ you can play a full and active role in your community;

◆ you can vote in national elections;

◆ you can apply for a UK passport.

Do you still need to sit a test? It depends on when you became a resident and whether or not you've taken the test. Anyone who was granted settlement before 2nd April 2007 will have avoided the 'Life in the UK' test at that stage, but will have to take it in order to apply for citizenship. **Every would-be permanent resident or citizen has to take the 'Life in the UK' test – but only once.**

You can apply for citizenship after living in the UK for a qualifying period, which is usually five years – or three years in the case of a husband, wife, or civil or same-sex partner (spouse). During this time, you should have been granted settlement (ILR) at least one year before applying for citizenship.

Other requirements include:

♦ being aged 18 or over – children can apply but there are different conditions;

♦ being of good character – checks will be made that you've paid your income tax and national insurance contributions, whether you have any civil or criminal convictions, and whether you've filed for bankruptcy. Black marks in this category account for around 10 per cent of rejections.

♦ being of sound mind – this means being able to make your own decisions;

♦ intending to stay in the UK – you're unlikely to be granted citizenship if you admit you're planning to live outside Britain.

In addition to all of the above, you must have passed the 'Life in the UK' test.

The timing of your application is important. You must have been present in the UK on the same day five years before you make your application (three years if applying as a spouse or partner), which is the date the Home Office receives your application. Therefore if you're stamped into the UK on 1st January 2004, you cannot apply before 1st January 2009 (or 2007 if you're a spouse). Check the arrival stamp date in your passport.

In addition, you should not have been absent from the UK for more than 90 days in each year, which is a total of 450 days in a five-year qualifying period or 270 days in a three-year qualifying period. Your number of days' absence in the year prior to your application is especially important.

Around 40 per cent of applications that are refused are due to a failure to meet these residency requirements – either the application has been made too early or the applicant has spent too much time outside the UK.

The citizenship application form is notoriously complicated! For a small fee (£40 in mid-2008), the Nationality Checking Service (NCS) will check your application form and supporting documents and copy any which you need to retain. This is especially useful if you need to use your passport during the two or three months that you're waiting for an answer. Many local councils also provide this service. For

more information, see 🖳 www.bia.homeoffice.gov.uk/britishcitizenship/applying/
checkingservice.

Citizenship is bestowed at a special ceremony, where you pledge loyalty to the United Kingdom, take the oath of allegiance to the Monarch (the Queen), and receive your certificate of citizenship. There's a government helpline where you can obtain more information about citizenship/naturalisation (☎ 0845-010 5200).

Note that if you're a citizen of another country and wish to retain that citizenship, then you must ensure that your country of origin won't revoke your citizenship if you become a UK citizen. The UK allows dual citizenship, i.e. being a citizen of two countries at the same time, but some countries don't.

Official figures reveal that around 60 per cent of people who are granted permanent residency go on to apply for citizenship. In 2006, this led to 150,000 passports being issued to new UK citizens.

Six Steps to Citizenship

Step 1: Decide that you want to become a UK citizen.

Step 2: Check your qualifying period and other requirements.

Step 3: Take the 'Life in the UK' test if you haven't already done so.

Step 4: Complete the form and apply for citizenship.

Step 5: Attend a citizenship ceremony.

Step 6: Receive your certificate – you're now a British citizen!

In mid-2008, the UK government was revising its immigration rules, and it may be that the immigration categories will change in future, as well as some of the requirements and qualifying periods, for both settlement and citizenship. It's unlikely that any of these changes will make it any more difficult for you to live in the UK, provided you have a genuine reason and are sufficiently skilled in the language and culture to live there successfully. For the most up-to-date information, check the UK Borders Agency's website (🖳 www.ukba.homeoffice. gov.uk).

IS THERE ANYONE WHO DOESN'T TAKE THE TEST?

There are always exceptions, but these are mostly based on age, disability – or being European! People from countries in the European Economic Area (EEA) don't need a visa to live or work in the UK. This includes all 27 European Union (EU) member countries, plus Iceland, Liechtenstein and Norway. Swiss nationals are treated the same as EEA nationals. The reason for this is that the European Charter lays down rules about the free movement of labour, therefore Britain cannot impose the 'Life in the UK' test on EEA or Swiss nationals. **However, EU and EEA nationals must take the test if they want to become British citizens.**

Other exemptions include children aged under 18 and people aged over 65, although they must provide proof of their age. Anyone who has a physical or mental impairment severe enough to prevent them from taking the test or studying an ESOL (English for Speakers of Other Languages) course may also be exempt, although test centres can cater for people with disabilities, such as limited mobility or visual impairment. If you fall into this category, you must provide adequate medical evidence to support the reason why you cannot take the test.

There are a few other groups who may not need to take the test. For more information see the UK Border Agency's website (⌨ www.ukba.homeoffice.gov.uk/ukresidency/settlement/applicationtypes) or call the Immigration and Nationality Enquiry Bureau's helpline (☎ 0870-606 7766).

ARE YOU READY TO TAKE THE TEST?

The 'Life in the UK' test consists of 24 multiple-choice questions based on the Home Office's *Life in the United Kingdom: A Journey to Citizenship* handbook. The pass mark is around 75 per cent, therefore you must get at least 18 questions right in order to pass. Bear this in mind

as you work through the practice questions in this book – and the practice questions in other books. If you aren't getting an average of 75 per cent correct, then you may not be ready to take the test.

There are around 400 questions in the 'Life in the UK' test question bank. There's no way of knowing which questions you will be asked – and the UK government keeps the formula secret – therefore none of the practice questions which you read in books (such as this one) are ever exactly the same as the real thing. If you memorise the questions, you may fail, but if you memorise the text the questions are based on, you have a good chance of passing.

The 'Life in the UK' test is intended to be taken by someone with a sufficient level of English, i.e. it's designed to test your English skills. If your English isn't good enough, you can instead take a language course which combines English studies with citizenship. The standard of English required to sit the test is called 'ESOL Entry 3'. ESOL stands for English for Speakers of Other Languages and Entry 3 refers to a level of competence that's sufficient to understand the test questions and the book on which they're based – the Home Office's *Life in the United Kingdom: A Journey to Citizenship* handbook.

So is your English good enough? If you can understand and use the tutorial on the 'Life in the UK' test website (⌨ www.lifeintheuktest.gov.uk), then you should have no problem with the test. You should also be able to read and understand this book. If not, you may need to enrol on an ESOL with citizenship course. These are offered at colleges of further education throughout the UK or call the 'Life in the UK' Helpline (☎ 0800-015 4245), which can advise you about courses in your area and where you can have your knowledge of English assessed.

Once you've completed the course successfully you receive a certificate that's accepted as proof of your knowledge of 'Life in the UK' and the English language, with no need to take a further test.

You can only take the 'Life in the UK' test in English. It isn't available in other 'foreign' languages – it's intended to check your English skills, after all! However, if you sit the test in Wales you can request to take it in Welsh, and in Scotland it's available in Scottish Gaelic, but you need to arrange this in advance.

How to Book your 'Life in the UK' Test

There are over 90 test centres around the UK – you can also find your nearest centre via the 'Life in the UK' website (⌨ www.lifeintheuktest.gov.uk) by selecting the 'Find a test centre' option in the top left-hand corner and entering your postcode.

You must wait a minimum of seven days for a test slot, which can be as long as four weeks during busy times, therefore if you're in a hurry try a different centre (you don't need to take the test at the centre closest to your home). If you have a disability, which means you need extra support to take the test (e.g. visual impairment or walking difficulties), inform the test centre staff when booking your test. The test costs £34 – there may be an administration fee of £10 if you cancel your test within seven days of the test date.

As well as the test fee, you must take some photo identification with you, such as one of the following:

♦ your passport;

♦ a UK photocard driving licence;

♦ a Home Office document, e.g. a Convention Travel Document (CTD), a Certificate of Identity Document (CID) or a Stateless Person Document (SPD);

♦ an Immigration Status Document, endorsed with a UK residence permit with your photograph.

You will be asked your full name, date of birth, nationality, country and place of birth, as well as your UK postcode and, if applicable, your Home Office reference. You may also be asked your reason for taking the test.

You take the test on a computer, which can be a bit daunting if you've never used one before. If this is the case, it's advisable to practise first on a friend's computer or at an internet café. In England you can contact UK Online (💻 www.ukonlinecentres.com/consumer) for details of centres that provide access to computers and the internet. Most local libraries also offer free or cheap internet access.

The 'Life in the UK' website (💻 www.lifeintheuktest.gov.uk) has a tutorial which takes you through the test step by step and also provides detailed instructions on how to use a mouse and keyboard. It's easier than it looks – even elderly people are surfing the internet these days (called 'silver surfers').

What Happens on Test Day?

When you arrive at the test centre, you show your photo ID to the test supervisor and pay for the test. You'll then be logged on to a computer and, after a short practice session the test will begin. You can change the appearance of your computer screen to make it easier to read. You won't be on your own – several candidates usually take the test during the same session, which is good for moral support!

You will have 45 minutes to answer 24 questions, which gives you plenty of time to think carefully about your answers, and to check them thoroughly at the end. Each candidate is given a different set of questions, chosen at random by the computer, so don't even think about peering at your neighbour's screen – there's no opportunity to cheat.

There's no waiting around for the results – you will be told whether you've passed or not as soon as the test session is over.

Some of the questions will reflect the region of the UK where you live. For example, if you take the test in Scotland, Wales or Northern Ireland, it's quite likely you'll be asked some questions relevant to those regions. However, don't ignore the information on these regions if you're taking the test in England, or you may be caught out!

You're able to move backwards and forwards through the questions, therefore if you have difficulty answering one, you can come back to it later. Ensure that you've answered all the questions before you hit the 'finish' button and make sure you use all the time available. People with certain medical conditions are allowed extra time to complete the test.

What if You Fail?

Don't despair. If you fail the test you'll receive a results notification letter which will indicate which sections of the *Life in the United Kingdom* book you need to revise. After doing your revision you can book another test as soon as you're ready, but you must wait at least seven days before you can re-sit the test.

If you fail several times, it may be that you have insufficient English to fully understand the test, in which case you should arrange to take some ESOL (English for Speakers of Other Languages – see box below) classes before applying to take the test again.

You can take the test as many times as necessary in order to pass. You won't be deported, even if you fail several times – provided you have a valid visa. If your temporary residency is due to run out and you haven't managed to pass, you must apply for an extension, known as further leave to remain in the UK (FLR), in order to give yourself more time to take and pass the 'Life in the UK' test.

A total of 131,549 people passed the 'Life in the UK' test between January and October 2007, which was a large increase on the whole of 2006, when just 105,402 secured a pass mark.

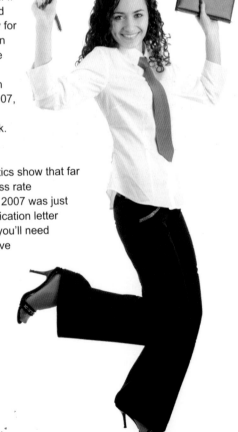

What if You Pass?

Congratulations! You're in the majority. Statistics show that far more candidates pass than fail. In fact the pass rate for the period between January and October 2007 was just over two-thirds. You will be given a pass notification letter to sign; this is an important document which you'll need when applying for citizenship or indefinite leave to remain, when the letter is attached to your application. The Home Office keeps a record of all those who've passed the test, but they don't keep your name on the list for ever, therefore don't leave it too long before applying.

Don't lose your pass notification letter – if you do you'll have to sit the test again!

HOW THIS BOOK CAN HELP YOU

The *Life in the UK: Test & Study Guide* was devised as an easy-to use revision guide to use alongside the Home Office's *Life in the United Kingdom: A Journey to Citizenship* handbook. We recommend that you read both books together. The 'Life in the UK' test is based upon chapters two to six of the Home Office's *Life in the United Kingdom*, and these same chapters are covered in this book, which reflects the key points of each chapter.

At the end of each chapter, there's a series of 60 questions designed to test your understanding of what you've just read. Answer the questions and look up the answers in the back of the book. If you've got at least 45 questions right then move on to the next section; if not, your knowledge is borderline, therefore you should go back and revise those parts of the chapter which you don't know well enough. Keep doing this until you're able to answer at least 75 per cent (45) of the questions in the book correctly. Once you can do this for all five chapters, you're ready to take the 'Life in the UK' test.

Good luck! You're about to become a permanent resident or citizen of Britain, a move that will change your life!

ESOL Classes

If you don't want to take the 'Life in the UK' test, you will need to gain an English for Speakers of Other Languages (ESOL) Entry Level 3 or above qualification, and can take an ESOL Skills for Life course (with at least 20 hours citizenship content). Make sure the ESOL course satisfies Home Office requirements for ESOL with Citizenship Context, and is accredited by a recognised awarding body approved by the Department of Innovation, Universities and Skills (DIUS), You can check with the Life in the UK Test website, the UK Border Agency or directly with DIUS.

2.
A CHANGING SOCIETY

This chapter is about the different people who've come to Britain, their reasons for moving here, and how this pattern of immigration has changed over the years. It also looks at the position of women in UK society, and how children and young people fit into British life.

MIGRATION TO BRITAIN

For many centuries, the UK has been a major destination for migrants – people who leave their own country to move to a new one. Many people living in Britain today can trace their roots to far-flung places, from Europe and the Middle East to Africa, Asia and the Caribbean. In the distant past, Britain was invaded by tribes from Europe and beyond, such as the Celts, Romans, Vikings and Saxons, who appropriated (took) land and property and decided to stay. In recent decades, people have migrated to Britain to join their families or find work, to escape persecution and to enjoy a better life.

Britain has a long history of opening its doors to people in danger, especially those facing persecution (mistreatment) for their ethnic background or choice of religion, as well as those suffering economic hardship. In particular, Britain welcomed the following three groups:

The Huguenots: "We were French Protestants who came to Britain in the 16th and 18th centuries. We were being persecuted in France because of our religious beliefs."

The Irish: "There was a terrible famine in Ireland in the 1840s. The potato crop failed and people were starving. We migrated to Britain and worked as labourers, helping to build the new canals and railways."

The Jews: "We were the victims of 'pogroms' (racist attacks) in our home country and we came to Britain seeking safety between 1880 and 1910. Our home country was the Russian Empire, although you might know it better as present-day Russia, Belarus, the Ukraine and Poland."

Migration Since 1945

Britain's infrastructure suffered a lot of damage during both world wars, both through bombing

must know

- The reasons why people have migrated to Britain.

- The groups of immigrants who came to the UK seeking work and safety between the 15th and 20th centuries – and why they came.

- Emigrants are people who leave their home country, while immigrants are people who move into a new country.

and the lack of manpower – many young men left to fight abroad. After the Second World War, a large part of the country needed to be rebuilt and industry restarted. Britain had lost many men during the war, and there weren't enough to do the work, so the government encouraged workers from other countries to come and help rebuild the UK.

Among those encouraged to come and work in Britain were people from Ireland and other parts of Europe, as well as the first waves of migrants from the West Indies (countries such as Jamaica, Barbados and Grenada, also known as the Caribbean islands), who began to take up the UK government's invitation in 1948. There was still a huge shortage of labour, which led to immigration being encouraged for economic reasons.

must know

⚡ The First World War took place from 1914 to 1918.

⚡ The Second World War took place from 1939 to 1945.

During the '50s, a lot of British industries, such as engineering, transport and textiles, actually advertised their job vacancies abroad. The new workers who responded to these recruitment drives became the basis of what are now Britain's largest ethnic groups, and their descendents are an important part of the UK's culture.

Bus drivers: "I was living in the West Indies when I saw jobs advertised to drive buses in Britain. I'd always wanted to visit the UK and I needed work, so I applied, and here I am driving the no. 67."

Textile workers: "I come from a village in India. Life was hard and we didn't have much to eat, so when an agent came to hire people to work in a clothing factory in the Midlands, I said yes. Many work colleagues come from India and Pakistan. Other friends went to work in engineering firms in the north of England."

Factory workers: "I live in the north of England. My grandparents came from Pakistan in the '50s to work for a large engineering firm. My parents were born here, and so was I. I've never been Pakistan. I'd like to visit, but all my friends are here in the UK."

People from the West Indies, India and Pakistan continued to settle and work in Britain for the next 25 years. Later, citizens of Bangladesh (formerly East Pakistan) joined the wave of immigrants. At the end of the '60s there were fewer migrants, although not everyone in the UK welcomed them with open arms, and in the early '70s the British government passed new laws which placed restrictions (limits) on immigration. A few exceptions were made: for example, people from countries in the 'old' Commonwealth, which included Australia, New Zealand and Canada, didn't face such strict controls.

Britain continued to offer a place of refuge to refugees – people who face danger in their country of origin, due to war, political reasons or persecution – which led to two more waves of immigration in the '70s.

Ugandan Asians: "We are people of Indian origin who lived in Uganda in Africa. In 1972, thousands of us were forced to leave Uganda by the dictator Idi Amin and, luckily, we were able to start again in Britain."

South-east Asians: "We lived in Vietnam, but were in great danger because of the Vietnam War in the late '70s. More than 25,000 south-east Asians have settled in Britain since 1979."

Migration at the End of the 20th Century

In the '80s, Britain's largest numbers of immigrants were coming from the most prosperous western countries, such as the United States (US), as well as from Australia, New Zealand and South Africa. However, in the early '90s, groups of people from the former Soviet Union started arriving in the UK. Like immigrants before them from east and west, they were looking for a safer and more prosperous way of life.

There is no end to the popularity of migration and, in fact, there's been a huge rise in mass global migration since 1994, with people throughout the world moving to new countries for economic and political reasons. A great many still favour the UK as their number one choice.

- Some of the reasons why people immigrated to the UK: for example, to escape danger or economic problems, or to work.
- The kinds of jobs that the Irish migrants did.
- The reasons why immigrants were invited to come to Britain after 1945, who was invited and the sort of work they did.
- The main immigrant groups who've come to Britain since 1945.
- Where Britain recruited workers from in the '50s.
- How immigration changed in the late '60s.
- The two immigrant groups who were invited to seek safety in the UK in the '70s.
- How mass migration changed in the '90s.

THE CHANGING ROLE OF WOMEN

Families in 19th-century Britain were large, and everyone worked long hours. In poorer homes, the whole family – men, women and children – had to work and contribute to the household income. In more wealthy families, women were far less likely to work; however, they also had far fewer rights than men.

- ◆ Until **1857**, a married woman had no right to divorce her husband.
- ◆ Until **1882**, when a couple married the woman's earnings, property and money automatically became her husband's property.

Towards the end of the 19th century and the beginning of the 20th century, women started to protest about this unfair treatment. They demonstrated and campaigned for greater rights; most of all they wanted the right to vote. This is known as 'suffrage' and so the women were called 'Suffragettes'. They marched through cities, chained themselves to railings and went on hunger strike to get their point across. One even threw herself in front of the King's racehorse at a famous horse race, the Epsom Derby.

How Women Won their Equality

Ironically, it was the outbreak of the First World War that began to change women's lives and make them more independent. Women won a certain amount of equality by joining the 'war effort' when they were required to do new and different work – men's work – while men were away fighting. They worked on farms and in factories and kept the country going, which continued after the war as Britain was still short of male workers, having lost huge numbers of young men on the battlefields of Europe.

The war ended in 1918, when women aged over 30 were finally given the right to vote and to stand for election to Parliament. However, they had to wait another ten years, until 1928, before they were allowed to vote at age 21 – the same age as men.

Although the situation had improved for women, they still didn't have equal rights with men. In particular, they faced discrimination (different and unfair treatment) at work. Many people (usually men) still believed that a woman's place was in the home and that they shouldn't go out to work. It wasn't unusual for an employer to ask a female worker to leave her job as soon as she got married.

At the same time, many jobs weren't available to women, often the same jobs that female workers had done during the war. Education, too, discriminated against women, and it was hard for a female student to secure a place at university.

During the '60s and '70s, women fought much harder for equal rights. This became known as 'women's liberation' (setting women free) or women's lib for short. Eventually, new laws were passed which gave women access to equal pay and prohibited (banned) employers from discriminating against workers just because they were female. There's more information on this in **Chapter 6 Employment** on page 145.

Women in Britain Today

In 21st century Britain, women make up 51 per cent of the population and 45 per cent of the workforce. There are some important differences between men and women:

♦ Girls now leave school with better qualifications than boys.

♦ There are now more women than men at university.

♦ Three-quarters of women with school-age children work.

Although many women still work in traditional female areas, such as healthcare, teaching, secretarial and office work, retail and shop work, there's an ever-increasing range of employment opportunities available to women. They can be doctors, lawyers and even engineers – roles that were closed to them in the past. They can even be Prime Minister, as Margaret Thatcher proved in the '80s!

must know

• Women's situation in the 19th century – in which years they were given the right to divorce and to keep their own property.

• The 'Suffragettes' – who they were and what they wanted.

• When women received the right to vote and stand for election in Parliament – this happened in two stages and in different years.

• How women campaigned in the '60s and '70s and won the right to equal pay and the end of sex discrimination.

There's strong evidence that attitudes to women are changing. Research shows that few people now believe that women in Britain should stay at home and not go out to work. Women probably work harder than ever before. Even those who go out to work still do the majority of the housework and childcare. Fortunately, men are taking more responsibility for looking after children, and are now more likely to help with the housework also.

Complete sexual equality is still some way off. There are laws against discrimination against women, especially in the workplace, although it still exists, and there's still work to be done to achieve greater equality of the sexes. Even in the 21st century, female workers don't always have the same access as men to promotion, and may miss out on better-paid jobs. Meanwhile, women still earn less than men. On average, the hourly pay rate for a woman is 20 per cent less than for a man, and even if she has a degree from a top university, she may still earn less than some of her male colleagues.

ᗺ The percentage of the UK's population that is female.

ᗺ The percentage of the UK's workforce that is female.

ᗺ That 75 per cent of women with school-age children also work.

ᗺ How girls' exam results at school compare with boys' – and how women do at university compared with men.

ᗺ Whether most people think women should stay at home – or go to work.

ᗺ Who does most of the housework and childcare.

CHILDREN, FAMILY & YOUNG PEOPLE

In Britain, there are almost 15m children and young people aged under 19, who make up almost a quarter of the population. They represent Britain's future, and their attitudes and aspirations (desires) are what will shape the next few decades.

Family life has changed a great deal during the last 20 years, as attitudes towards divorce and separation have softened. Both are now considered a normal part of life, so much so that the traditional mum, dad and 2.4 children nuclear family model is struggling to survive.

In today's Britain:

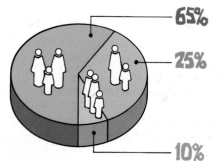

65%

65 per cent of children live with both of their birth parents

25%

25 per cent live in a lone-parent family

10 per cent live within a step-family (a family where either the mother or father is not the biological parent of one or more of the children)

10%

Most UK children receive weekly pocket money from their parents, and some also earn extra money by doing chores (jobs) around the home. Now that most mothers work, this extra help is useful. Children's lifestyles have also changed. British children used to play in parks and on the street, but they don't play outside home as much as they used to. This is because:

♦ There are now more home-based forms of entertainment, including television, DVDs and computers.

♦ There is growing concern for the safety of children, due to increased reports in newspapers about children being molested (sexually attacked) by strangers. In fact, there's no evidence that there has been an increase in such incidents.

As they grow up, young people live different lives from the older generation. They wear different, more informal, clothes; they also have different interests and identities; even the language they use to express themselves is often very different from that of the older generation.

Britain's young people are often independent and tend to leave the family home when they become adults, keen to have a job and a home of their own, although this doesn't happen in all communities – Asian youngsters, for example, are more likely to stay at home for longer.

Children in Education

By law, all children between the ages of 5 and 16 must attend school. Their education comprises lessons on a set number of subjects decided by the government, known as the National Curriculum. Their progress is assessed by teachers at certain ages and there are also tests, known as examinations. These vary according to where children live:

must know

↻ That a quarter of the UK's population is aged 19 or younger.

↻ There are around 15m children under 19 in the UK.

↻ The percentage of children who live with both of their birth parents, and those who don't.

↻ How children receive pocket money from their parents, and the way in which their playtime has changed.

↻ That once they become adults, most children tend to leave the family home.

♦ In England and Scotland, children take national tests in English, mathematics and science at the ages of 7, 11 and 14.

♦ In Wales, children are assessed (measured) by their teachers at ages 7 and 11 and then tested at 14.

These tests and assessments provide information about children's educational progress, which subjects they're doing well in, and where they need more help. Examinations are major markers in young peoples' lives, the most important of which are listed below:

♦ **GCSE** – General Certificate of Secondary Education, which is taken at the age of 16. Remember the initials by learning this phrase: Get Caught Stealing Eggs.

- ♦ **SQA** – Scottish Qualifications Authority Standard Grade examinations are the Scottish equivalent of the GCSE, also taken at 16. Remember it this way: Silently Queuing Ants.

- ♦ **AGCE** – General Certificate of Education at an Advanced level. These exams, which used to be known as A Levels, are taken at the age of 17 or 18. Remember it this way: A Giant Cream Egg.

- ♦ **AS** – Advanced Subsidiary level. This is the equivalent of half an AGCE. While an AGCE is made up of six units, the AS level (remember it by Angry Squirrel) has three. If a student goes on to take a further three units of the course, the qualification then becomes an AGCE.

- ♦ **Higher/Advanced Higher Grades** – These are the Scottish equivalent of AS levels and AGCEs, although they can't be directly compared. Higher Grades are taken first and Advanced Higher Grades follow.

Children take GCSEs and SQAs at school. If they get good enough grades they can then go on to take AGCEs, AS levels or Higher/Advanced Higher courses either at school or at a college. Alternatively, they can take a vocational (trade or career) qualification.

Traditionally, higher education institutions (such as universities) select students based on their AGCE grades, but these days students entering universities tend to have a variety of qualifications.

Studying After School

Today, a third of all young people go on to higher education, either at a college or a university. The government would like to see more taking this option, and has set a target at 50 per cent. However, higher education can

must know

- ⟳ The ages at which education is compulsory in the UK.

- ⟳ When, how and why children's learning is assessed, and how this differs in different regions of the UK.

- ⟳ Which examinations young people take at the age of 16.

- ⟳ Which examinations young people take at the age of 17 or 18.

- ⟳ The different examinations in Scotland.

be expensive, and there's pressure on young people and their families to pay both university fees and their living costs while they continue their studies.

Some students take a year out of education before going to university – known as a 'gap year'. They may spend this time travelling abroad (e.g. backpacking) or doing voluntary work in the UK or another country. However, they're just as likely to spend the time working to earn money to fund their next few years at university.

⤷ How many young people go on to college or university.

⤷ What a gap year is. The different examinations in Scotland.

In Britain, qualifications are not just for the young. People aged over 16 can study a wide range of academic and vocational courses at Colleges of Further Education or Adult Education Centres. Courses in leisure interests and skills are also available, from pottery and other handicrafts to massage and foreign languages. Contact your local college for details.

There's more information on education in **Chapter 5, Everyday Needs**, on page 101.

Children at work

British children start earning a living early, and many have a part-time job before or after school – it's thought that up to 2m are working at any one time. Parents often support their children working, as they believe it teaches them about being independent. It also gives the kids extra income, and in poorer families their income may be a much-needed boost to family finances.

Typical jobs include working in a newsagent's (a shop which sells newspapers and magazines) and delivering newspapers to people's homes, as well as working in supermarkets. However, there are strict laws about what work children can and cannot do, the age at which they can take up paid work and the number of hours they can work. In most instances they must be aged over 14 before they can take a job, and the law regulates the work they do and the number of hours they can work. For more information, see the Worksmart website (🖳 www.worksmart.org.uk).

There are concerns for the safety of children who work illegally or without supervision, and their employment is strictly controlled.

Health Hazards

It's during their teenage years that many young people are susceptible to peer-pressure which pushes them into the misuse of alcohol, drugs and tobacco. Parents tend to worry about their children using these substances, and the following facts appear to justify their fears.

⤷ Many school-age children have a part-time job.

⤷ How the government safeguards working children, e.g. with a minimum working age.

⤷ Places where it's legal for children to work.

Smoking

As more and more adults quit smoking, so statistics show that more teenagers are taking it up, and school-age girls smoke more than boys of the same age. The government is pushing hard to reduce the number of teenage and young smokers – and smokers in general. From October 1st 2007, it's been illegal to sell tobacco products to under-18s, and smoking is mostly banned in public buildings and workplaces across the UK.

Alcohol

It's illegal for a shop-keeper to sell alcohol to under-18s, who also aren't allowed to buy it. However, it's a fact that many young people not only start drinking alcohol before they're 18, but that some find it hard to control their alcohol intake. There's considerable concern about teenagers (and adults) who 'binge drink' – consuming a high number of alcoholic drinks in one session. Friday nights in some town and city centres are notorious for groups of drunken teenagers. In fact, it's illegal to be drunk in public – regardless of how old you are – and there are penalties such as on-the-spot fines.

Illegal drugs

As in most countries, in Britain it's illegal to possess or sell certain drugs, such as cannabis, heroin, cocaine, ecstasy and amphetamines. Even so, drug abuse is a serious problem, and statistics show that half of all young adults, and around a third of the entire population, have used illegal drugs at one time or another, even if they aren't habitual (regular) users.

There's a strong link between the use of hard drugs (such as crack cocaine and heroin) and crime, because drug addicts often turn to burglary and mugging (violent theft from a person) to obtain money to buy drugs. The link is equally strong between hard drugs and mental illness. Drug abuse has serious social and financial costs for the UK, and society needs to find a way to deal with the problem.

Young Peoples' Political & Social Attitudes

Although young people in Britain can vote in elections from the age of 18, many don't. In the 2001 general election, for example, only 20 per cent of first-time voters used their vote. Politicians have had long debates about why new voters aren't interested in voting, and many think young adults just aren't interested in the political process. However, while young adults

must know

- ⟳ That smoking is on the increase among young adults, especially girls.
- ⟳ It's illegal to sell cigarettes or alcohol to under-18s.
- ⟳ It's illegal to be drunk in public.
- ⟳ The percentage of young adults who've tried illegal drugs.
- ⟳ The links between hard drugs, crime and mental illness.

may not be lapping up all the party politics that comes out of Westminster, they do take an interest in specific political issues, such as the environment (green issues) and animal cruelty.

A survey in 2003 among young people in England and Wales found that the five things they rated the most important issues in Britain were:

♦ crime

♦ drugs

♦ war/terrorism

♦ racism

♦ health

The same survey asked them about taking part in political and community events. It revealed that in spite of their apparent disinterest in voting, an impressive 86 per cent of young people had been involved in a community event in the preceding year, and that half had taken part in fund-raising or collected money for charity. Similar trends have been found in Scotland and Northern Ireland. Many children first become involved in such activities at school while studying citizenship as part of the National Curriculum.

must know

⟳ The age that young people can vote.

⟳ The percentage which used their vote in the 2001 general election.

⟳ The political issues which most young people are interested in.

⟳ Young peoples' involvement in community issues and charity events.

WORDS TO LEARN

Check that you understand this chapter's key words and terms:

Migration to Britain

migrate, immigrate, immigration, immigrant
persecution, famine, conflict
labour, labourer
recruit
restrict
political asylum
the war effort

Changing Role of Women

income, earnings
rights, equal rights
campaign, demonstrate
discriminate, discrimination
prohibit
workforce
household
promotion

Children, Family & Young People

eligible
concern
molestation
attitudes
hazards
birth parent, step-family
compulsory
informal

methods of assessment
defer
gap year
independent
income
misuse
addictive substances
abuse
binge drinking
on-the-spot fines
controlled drugs
criminal offence
possess
heroin, cocaine, crack cocaine, ecstasy,
  amphetamines, cannabis
burglary, mugging
debate
politicians, political process, party politics,
political issues
specific
concern
environment
terrorism, racism
participation
fund-raising

PRACTICE QUESTIONS

Now test your knowledge of Britain's changing society with these practice questions. Make sure you can answer them all before you take your test.

1. **Which people did Britain offer safety to in the 16th and 18th centuries, when they were** being persecuted in their home country?

    A   French
    B   Huguenots
    C   Jews
    D   Saxons

2. **In the 19th century, Britain was invaded by tribes from Europe and beyond, who took land and stayed. True or false?**

3. **Where did Britain set up recruitment centres for bus drivers in the '50s?**

    A   France
    B   Ireland
    C   The West Indies
    D   Pakistan

4. **Irish immigrants helped to build Britain's railways and canals. True or false?**

5. **At what time, in recent history, did Britain need to recruit large numbers of workers from abroad?**

    A   After the First World War
    B   After the Falklands War
    C   After the Gulf War
    D   After the Second World War

6. **In the '50s, what were people from India and Pakistan recruited to do?**

    A   Build railways
    B   Work in potteries
    C   Work in textile and engineering firms
    D   Build roads

7. **Which people came to Britain in the 1840s because of a famine at home?**

    A   The Portuguese
    B   The Irish
    C   The Huguenots
    D   The Polish

8. The Jews came to Britain from the Ottoman Empire. True or false?

9. The Second World War took place from 1938 to 1945. True or false?

10. From the '50s onwards, for how many years did people from the West Indies, India and Pakistan steadily immigrate into Britain?

    A   25 years
    B   10 years
    C   50 years
    D   15 years

11. When did the British government pass laws which restricted immigration?

    A   1980s
    B   2000
    C   1960s
    D   1950s

12. In the '80s, which countries were the largest group of immigrants coming from?

    A   India and Bangladesh
    B   Uganda and Vietnam
    C   Ireland
    D   The US, Australia, New Zealand and South Africa

13. The Indians who migrated to Britain from Africa in 1972 had been living in Kenya. True or false?

14. During the late 19th century, where did Jewish people come from in search of a safer life?

    A   The former Russian Empire
    B   Pakistan
    C   Iraq
    D   The former Yugoslavia

15. What reasons have there been for a global rise in mass migration since 1994? Give two answers.

    A   Widespread famine
    B   Political reasons
    C   Cheaper airfares
    D   Economic reasons

16. There hasn't been a global rise in mass migration since 1994. True or false?

17. In which year did women get the right to divorce their husbands?

    A   1857
    B   1836
    C   1957
    D   1914

18. What name was given to the group of women who campaigned for the right to vote?

    A   The Busy Bees
    B   Worthy Women
    C   Voting Right
    D   The Suffragettes

19. Before 1882, married women's earnings, property and money automatically belonged to their husbands. True or false?

20. A man didn't automatically own his wife's money and property before 1882. True or false?

21. In which year were women over 30 given the right to vote?

    A   1890
    B   1980
    C   1945
    D   1918

22. Women could vote at the same age as men in 1925? True or false?

23. Women were given the right to vote at the age of 21 in 1928. True or false?

24. How much less than men do women earn today for an hour's work?

    A   15 per cent
    B   20 per cent
    C   30 per cent
    D   10 per cent

25. What percentage of women with school-age children work today?

    A   90 per cent
    B   75 per cent
    C   50 per cent
    D   10 per cent

26. If a working woman married in the '50s, her employer sometimes asked her to leave her job. True or false?

27. In which two decades did women fight hard for equal rights?

    A   1850s and 1860s
    B   1960s and 1970s
    C   1920s and 1930s
    D   1980s and 1990s

28. Women make up 45 per cent of the population and 51 per cent of the workforce. True or false?

29. There are now more women than men at university. True or false?

30. Most people no longer believe that women in Britain should stay at home and not go out to work. True or false?

31. Who does the majority of the housework?

    A   Men
    B   Women
    C   Children
    D   Cleaners

32. Girls do worse at school than boys. True or false?

33. How many people in the UK are aged under 19?

    A   15 million
    B   25 million
    C   30 million
    D   23 million

34. What percentage of children lives with both of their birth parents?

    A   40 per cent
    B   75 per cent
    C   65 per cent
    D   90 per cent

35. A third of all children live in a lone-parent family. True or false?

36. **How often do most children receive pocket money from their parents?**

    A   Monthly
    B   Daily
    C   Fortnightly
    D   Weekly

37. **Why don't children play outside the home as much as they used to? Give two answers.**

    A   They prefer to play on their computer
    B   They don't like the rain
    C   They are too busy working
    D   Their parents are concerned for their safety

38. **Young people tend not to stay in the family home when they become adults. True or false?**

39. **Until what age does the law say that children must attend school?**

    A   15
    B   18
    C   16
    D   17

40. **Children are tested or assessed in which subjects at the ages of seven, 11 and 14?**

    A   History, geography and geology
    B   English, maths and science
    C   French, maths and English
    D   Citizenship, geography and science

41. **What does GCSE stand for?**

    A   General Certificate of School Education
    B   Graded Children of Significant Education
    C   Great Children of Scotland and England
    D   General Certificate of Secondary Education

42. **Which examinations do children take at the age of 16? Give two answers.**

    A   GCSE
    B   AGCE
    C   ABC
    D   SQA

43. At what age do children take AGCEs or AS levels in England, or Higher/ Advanced Higher courses in Scotland?

   A   11 and 12
   B   15 and 16
   C   17 and 18
   D   18 and 19

44. A quarter of young people go on to higher education. True or false?

45. What do most young people tend to do during a 'gap' year?

   A   Take more exams
   B   Work and travel
   C   Community service
   D   Look after their family

46. At what age are children normally allowed to start a part-time job?

   A   14
   B   12
   C   16
   D   15

47. It's legal for a 14 year old to work in a bar. True or false.

48. It's illegal to sell tobacco products to people under what age?

   A   16
   B   20
   C   18
   D   21

49. Smoking is on the increase among young people. True or false?

50. What is the legal drinking age in the UK?

   A   15
   B   16
   C   17
   D   18

51. It's illegal to be drunk in your own home. True or false?

52. **Half of young adults have used illegal drugs at one time or another. True or false?**

53. **What are hard drugs strongly linked to? Give two answers.**

    A   Mental illness
    B   Increased intelligence
    C   Burglary and mugging
    D   Gaining weight

54. **It's illegal to possess which drugs?**

    A   Heroin, cocaine, ecstasy, amphetamines and cannabis
    B   Paracetamol and aspirin
    C   Anti-depressants
    D   Vitamins

55. **What proportion of the UK population as a whole has tried illegal drugs?**

    A   Three-quarters
    B   Half
    C   A third
    D   Two-thirds

56. **From what age can British people vote?**

    A   30
    B   18
    C   21
    D   16

57. **What percentage of first-time voters used their vote in the 2001 election?**

    A   20 per cent
    B   33 per cent
    C   50 per cent
    D   66 per cent

58. **Which political issues do young people consider most important? Give two answers.**

    A   Crime
    B   Restrictions on live music
    C   War/terrorism
    D   Corruption

59. In a 2003 survey, over 80 per cent of young people said they hadn't been involved in a community event in the preceding year. True or false?

60. In the same survey, what percentage of young people said that they had collected money or fund-raised in the preceding year?

    A   25 per cent
    B   75 per cent
    C   50 per cent
    D   15 per cent

The answers are on page 202.

Kettlewell, Yorkshire Dales

Piper, Glasgow, Scotland

3.
UK TODAY: A PROFILE

T his chapter is about the different people of the United Kingdom. It reveals the population in the four countries that make up the UK, and explains how population information is collected. It also looks at the different ethnic groups and the religions which people follow. Finally, it provides information about popular customs, traditions and sports that are typically British.

POPULATION

As in many countries, the UK's population is growing faster each year. Since 1971 it has increased by 7.7 per cent – in 2005, the population was just under 60m people. However, population growth is as much due to people migrating to the UK, as to an increase in the numbers already in Britain. The birth rate is falling, with fewer couples choosing to have children, and those that do are opting for smaller families. The death rate is also falling, as improvements in medical care enable people to live longer. There are more men and women aged over 60 than there are children under 16 and there's also a greater number of people aged over 85 than ever before.

Not every area of the UK shares the growth trend, which has seen the general population increase in the last 20 years. In the north-east and north-west, the numbers have actually declined.

SCOTLAND
5·1m 8%

NORTHERN
IRELAND
1·7m 3%

WALES
2·9m 5%

ENGLAND
50·1m 84%

TOTAL
59·8m

The Census

The census is an official count of a country's population, which also gathers information about peoples' age, place of birth, jobs, ethnicity, housing, health and marital status. The UK's first census took place in 1801; since then it's been taken every ten years, and the next one is due in 2011. The only time the census was missed was in 1941, due to the Second World War.

⌒ The census has been taken every ten years since 1801 and the next one is due in 2011.

⌒ All information collected is kept confidential for 100 years.

The information gathered in the census is used to identify population trends, and to help the government plan for the future. An increase in births means more schools will be needed, while a greater number of older people will require increased funding for medical care. The law states that every household must complete a census form. The information they give remains confidential and is only released to the public after 100 years; people sometimes use information from past censuses to research family history.

More information about the UK census, the form and population statistics can be found at 💻 www.statistics.gov.uk/census.

Ethnic Diversity

The UK is made up of four separate countries (England, Scotland, Wales and Northern Ireland – sometimes referred to, incorrectly, as Ulster), each with its own customs, attitudes and histories. The inhabitants of these countries are known as the English, the Scots, the Welsh and the Northern Irish. However, there are people from many more races living in the UK.

Britain is celebrated for its ethnic diversity, which is particularly evident in its larger cities and urban areas. Visit London, Manchester or Birmingham and you will see a truly multi-cultural Britain, but this mix of cultures is much less obvious in Scotland, Wales and Northern Ireland, or in more rural parts of England.

The UK population is changing and evolving rapidly, particularly in cities such as London, therefore it's difficult to get a precise picture of the exact ethnic origin of the entire population from census statistics. The most recent figures show that 8.3 per cent of the population is of Indian, Pakistani, Chinese, Black Caribbean, Black African, Bangladeshi and mixed ethnic descent. About half of this group is thought to have been born in the UK.

In addition to the main ethnic groups, there are also large numbers of Irish, Italian, Greek and Turkish Cypriot, Polish, Australian, Canadian, New Zealand and American people living in the UK today. In 2004, a number of Eastern European countries joined

the European Union (EU), and many Eastern Europeans have since made their home in the UK. In some areas, supermarkets sell Polish bread and sausages alongside Indian spices, Chinese noodles and Caribbean sauces.

Ethnic Groups

The following table shows the main ethnic groups as revealed by the National Statistics from the 2001 census.

Ethnic group	Millions (m)	% of population
White	54.2 m	92 per cent
Mixed	0.7 m	1.2 per cent
Asian or Asian British		
Indian	1.1 m	1.8 per cent
Pakistani	0.7 m	1.3 per cent
Bangladeshi	0.3 m	0.5 per cent
Other Asian	0.2 m	0.4 per cent
Black or Black British		
Black Caribbean	0.6 m	1.0 per cent
Black African	0.5 m	0.8 per cent
Black other	0.1 m	0.2 per cent
Chinese	0.2 m	0.4 per cent
Other	0.2 m	0.4 per cent

Where Do the Largest Ethnic Minority Groups Live?

Most of the UK's ethnically-descended population live in England – a far smaller number live in Scotland, Wales or Northern Ireland. The most multi-cultural city is London – 45 per cent of Britain's ethnic minority population is based in the Greater London area, where they make up almost a third (29 per cent) of the overall population. There are also large ethnic minority populations in Yorkshire, Humberside, the north-west, the west Midlands and the south-east.

The proportions of ethnic minority groups in the countries of the UK are as follows:

England	9 per cent
Scotland	2 per cent
Wales	2 per cent
Northern Ireland	less than 1 per cent

must know

- The countries which make up the UK, the people who live there and the proportions of ethnic minorities in the country.

- The ethnic minority groups which make up 8.3 per cent of Britain's population – the numbers, percentages and where they live.

- The proportion of ethnic minorities who were born in Britain.

- The smaller ethnic groups which also live in Britain.

- The ethnic make-up of Greater London, which is home to 45 per cent of the UK's ethnic population and where minorities make up 9 per cent of the population.

THE NATIONS & REGIONS OF THE UK

The UK is a medium-sized country and most of its people live in towns and cities. The longest distance you can travel on the UK mainland is from John O'Groats on the north coast of Scotland to Land's End at the most south-westerly tip of Cornwall – a distance of 870mi (1,400km).

Despite its relatively small size, Britain is home to a great many regional differences in culture and language. Different areas have different accents and even different dialects (varieties of language). Some of the best known are Geordie (spoken on Tyneside, the area around Newcastle), Scouse (Liverpool) and Cockney (East London). There are also regional variations in local customs, food and even architecture.

English is the UK's official language, but it's by no means the only one. In Wales, a growing number of people are learning and using Welsh. There are Welsh TV and radio channels, signs are written in Welsh, and the language is also taught in Welsh schools and universities.

Scotland and Northern Ireland both share a language called Gaelic. It's spoken in some parts of the Highlands and Islands

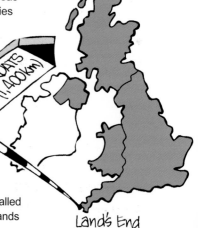

of northern Scotland, as well as in Northern Ireland, where it's known as Irish Gaelic. Some of the dialects of English spoken in Scotland reflect the old Scottish language called Scots, and in Northern Ireland there's a dialect known as Ulster Scots.

There are many more languages that have been brought to Britain by immigrants – including Urdu, Bengali, Punjabi, Polish, Turkish, Somali, Arabic and Mandarin Chinese – and you can hear them all in multi-cultural cities.

- ⤴ The furthest points north and south in the UK, and the distance between them.
- ⤴ Where most of the population lives.
- ⤴ The most important accents and dialects of the UK.
- ⤴ The regional languages of Scotland, Wales and Northern Ireland.
- ⤴ Other ways you can identify regional differences in the UK.

RELIGION

Throughout history, the UK has been a Christian society and has an 'established' church – the Church of England – but everyone is free to practise the religion of their choice. You're also free **not** to practise a religion, and a large number of British people claim to have no religion.

In the 2001 census, just over 75 per cent of the British population said that they had a religion, and of these, 70 per cent claimed to be Christians. However, only 10 per cent of the UK population attend a religious service of any kind. Those who live in Scotland and Northern Ireland are more likely to attend a religious service than those in England and Wales, although the number of people in London who do so is on the increase.

In spite of the dominance of Christianity, there are a lot of people in the UK who follow other religions. The most popular religions are:

- ◆ Christian   71.6% (10 per cent of Christians are Roman Catholic)
- ◆ Muslim   2.7%
- ◆ Hindu   1.0%
- ◆ Sikh   0.6%
- ◆ Jewish   0.5%
- ◆ Buddhist   0.3%
- ◆ Other   0.3%
- ◆ No religion   15.5%
- ◆ Not stated   7.3%

Source: National Statistics from the 2001 census.

Christian Churches

Although Britain has no official religion, there is a constitutional link (one set down in the system of government) between the church and the state. The UK's official church is the Church of England, called the Anglican Church in other countries, or the Episcopal Church in Scotland and the US. Established by King Henry VIII (8th) in the 1530s in a break away from the Pope and the Catholic religion – an era known as the Reformation – the Church of England is a Protestant church. The head or Supreme Governor of the church is the monarch (King or Queen) – currently Queen Elizabeth II (2nd). Because of the link with the church, the monarch isn't allowed to marry a Catholic.

must know

- The UK's attitude to freedom of religion.
- The percentage of people who say they have a religion, who claim to be Christian and who attend a religious service.
- The proportion of people who say they have no religion.
- What percentages of people are Muslim, Hindu, Sikh, Jewish or Buddhist.

The Church of England's spiritual leader is the Archbishop of Canterbury. Although the monarch has the right to appoint the Archbishop and other senior church officials, it's usually the Prime Minister and a committee appointed by the Church which makes this important decision. Some members of the House of Lords (see page 73) are Church of England bishops (Christian religious leaders).

Scotland's established church is the Presbyterian Church of Scotland, which is free from state control. The Scottish church is governed by a series of courts, and its most senior representative is the Moderator of its Annual General Assembly (meeting or gathering). There is no established church in Wales or Northern Ireland.

There are several other Protestant churches in the UK, which include Baptists, Presbyterians, Methodists and Quakers. The Roman Catholic Church is also important in the UK, where 10 per cent of Christians are Catholics (40 per cent in Northern Ireland).

Patron Saints

In Christianity, a patron saint is a saint (holy person) who has a special link with a group of people who believe that he or she is more likely to answer their prayers. Each of the UK's countries has their own patron saint, each of which has a feast day. In past times these were holy (sacred) days when people took time off work; today, the only saint's day that's taken as a public holiday is St Patrick's Day in Northern Ireland on the 17th March.

Patron Saints' Days

The four patron saints and their days are:

1st March	St David's Day	(Wales)
17th March	St Patrick's Day	(Northern Ireland)
23rd April	St George's Day	(England)
30th November	St Andrew's Day	(Scotland)

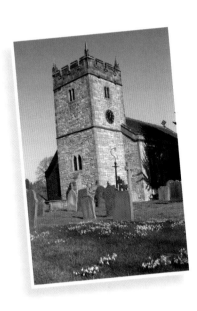

- The Church of England (Anglican Church) is the state (established) church in England.

- Who is the head of the Church of England, and who is its spiritual head.

- Scotland's established church is the Presbyterian Church of Scotland, while Wales and Northern Ireland have no established church.

- The percentage of Christians who are Roman Catholics.

- The different patron saints – and their saint's days – in England, Scotland, Wales and Northern Ireland.

Public Holidays

As in most Christian countries, many public holidays in the UK are religious holidays. There are eight public or bank holidays (so called because banks close) in England and Wales, which are listed below:

Public Holidays		
1st January	New Year's Day	National holiday
Last Friday before Easter	Good Friday	Religious holiday
First Monday after Easter	Easter Monday	Also a Bank Holiday but not in Scotland
First Monday in May	Early May Bank Holiday	
Last Monday in May	Spring Bank Holiday	
Last Monday in August	Late Summer Bank Holiday	
25th December	Christmas Day	Religious holiday
26th December	Boxing Day	National holiday

In addition, the Scots get an extra day off at New Year (2nd January) and St Andrews Day (around 30th November), and people in Northern Ireland take St Patrick's Day (17th March) and Orangemen's Day (to commemorate the Battle of the Boyne – 2 Monday in July) as holidays.

CUSTOMS & TRADITIONS

Festivals

There are festivals celebrated throughout the year in the UK. Some are celebrations of music, arts and culture, such as the Edinburgh Festival (an arts festival in Scotland's capital city) and the Notting Hill Carnival, a street festival of music and dance which takes place in west London. Easter and Christmas are important festivals which have their roots in the Christian religion, while New Year is a traditional celebration. Festivals of other religions are also widely recognised in Britain, such as Eid ul-Fitr (Muslim), Diwali (Hindu) and Hanukkah (Jewish), which children learn about in school.

A Year of Festivities

New Year

New Year starts on New Year's Eve (31st December) when people celebrate the end of the old year and the start of the new. They go out to parties or stay at home and watch special shows on television. Many people spend New Year's Day (1st January) recovering from the night before! New Year is especially important in Scotland, where 31st December is called Hogmanay and 2nd January is an extra public holiday. Hogmanay is a big deal in Scotland and a more important festival than Christmas.

Valentine's Day

February 14th is a day for lovers and couples, when they give each other gifts and cards, and may do something special, such as go for a meal or a weekend away. Some people send anonymous cards to a person they secretly admire.

Mother's Day

This falls on the Sunday three weeks before Easter, therefore it's on a different date each year. Children of all ages buy cards and gifts to show love and appreciation for their mothers, and may also cook a meal for her or take her out to dinner. Some people call it Mothering Sunday.

April Fool's Day

On 1st April, people play tricks on one another – but they can only do this until midday (noon). Newspapers, television and radio share the fun by reporting stories which are intended to deceive readers and audiences who've forgotten which day it is.

Easter

Easter is the most important Christian festival. It celebrates the resurrection of Jesus Christ after his death on Good Friday. The dates changes each year, but Good Friday falls on the first Friday after the first full moon on or after 21st March, with Easter Sunday two days later. The following Monday is also a holiday in most of the UK except Scotland.

Despite its religious roots, only a few people celebrate Easter by going to church on Good Friday and Easter Sunday. The majority have a secular celebration, during which they give each other chocolate Easter eggs. Some parents teach their children that, much like Father Christmas, the Easter Bunny delivers eggs overnight.

Symbols associated with Easter include Christian crosses and symbols of the new spring season, such as lambs, baby chicks and daffodils.

Halloween

Halloween has its roots in an ancient festival on 31st October called All Hallows Eve. Traditionally, it's the night when ghosts are out and about, which is represented by Halloween lanterns – hollow (empty) pumpkins with faces cut into them and lighted candles inside. Today, Halloween is influenced by America which invented 'trick or treating', where children dress up as scary characters such as witches and ghosts and knock on peoples' doors to ask, 'Trick or treat?' If you give them sweets, chocolates or money (a treat), the children will leave; if not, they may play a trick on you.

Guy Fawkes Night

The 5th November is Guy Fawkes Night, also called Bonfire Night, which people celebrate by lighting an open-air fire (bonfire) and setting off fireworks. Guy Fawkes was the leader of a group of Catholic rebels who in 1605 tried to kill the Protestant King by placing a bomb in the Houses of Parliament – this act of treason (a crime against a country) became known as the Gunpowder Plot. For this reason, children often make an effigy (dummy) of Guy Fawkes, called a 'Guy', which they burn on the bonfire.

> Use this children's rhyme to remember Guy Fawkes Night:
>
> "Remember, remember, the fifth of November, Gunpowder, treason and plot,
>
> We see no reason why Gunpowder Treason, Should ever be forgot!"

Remembrance Day

On 11th November, people remember those who died fighting during the First and Second World Wars, as well as in other wars. To mark the occasion, many people wear a poppy, a red flower which grew on the First World War battlefields in Belgium and France. There is a two-minute silence at 11am. A way to remember this date is to know that the First World War officially ended on the 11th hour of the 11th day of the 11th month (November).

Christmas Day

By far the biggest celebration of the year, Christmas Day is on 25th December. It's a Christian festival which celebrates the birth of Jesus Christ, and many people go to church on Christmas Eve (24th December) or on Christmas Day itself. Non-Christians also celebrate it. The entire UK stops work for Christmas, and preparations begin in early December or even before. People send Christmas cards to their friends and family, and decorate their homes – many have a decorated Christmas tree with lights. There are Christmas parties, and shops are busy as people buy gifts. On Christmas Day, families and friends get together at home to celebrate with a special meal called Christmas dinner, which traditionally includes turkey.

Christmas is a special time for children. They believe that Father Christmas or Santa Claus – traditionally depicted wearing a red suit and with a long white beard – visits their home on the night of Christmas Eve and brings them gifts. The day after Christmas Day (26th December) is also a public holiday, called Boxing Day or St. Stephens Day.

SPORT

Sport plays an important role in the life and culture of Britain. The most popular sports are football, rugby, tennis, golf and cricket, but sports fanatics (known as 'fans') take an interest in many more games. England, Scotland, Wales and Northern Ireland all have their own national teams for rugby and football – there's no one main team for the UK, although the four home nations compete as one (Great Britain) in the Olympics.

Important Sporting Events

Even people who aren't interested in sport may watch the following events, which are shown on British television:

- ◆ **The Grand National** – a tough steeplechase horse race over large fences, which takes place at Aintree in Liverpool in spring.

- ◆ **The FA Cup Final** – the final of the Football Association (FA) cup in May is the biggest football event of the year. There are equivalent tournaments in Scotland, Wales and Northern Ireland.

- ◆ **The Open golf championship** – the Open, as it's known, takes place in July on one of the UK's golf courses, and is one of only four major golf events and the only one held outside the US.

- ◆ **Wimbledon** – a two-week tennis tournament in south London played on grass. It's the oldest tennis championship in the world – one of four Grand Slam tournaments – but no British woman has won the singles title since 1977 and no British man since 1936!

must know

- ◌ When are the UK's public holidays – and what are Bank Holidays.

- ◌ Which religious and national festivals are celebrated in Britain – when do they take place and how are they celebrated.

- ◌ That some important festivals are Christian, but other religions' festivals are also recognised and children learn about them in school.

- ◌ The most popular sports and sporting events.

WORDS TO LEARN

Check that you understand this chapter's key terms:

Population

population
birth rate, death rate
decline
statistics
census
ethnicity
marital status
trends
funding
household
confidential
inhabitant
ethnic minority
ethnic diversity, ethnic origin, ethnic group, mixed ethnic descent
multi-cultural
urban, rural

The Nations & Regions of the UK

region, regional
accent, dialect
architecture
official

Religion

religion, religious service
society
established
Christian, Christianity
Muslim, Hindu, Sikh, Jewish, Buddhist
freedom of religion
Roman Catholic Church
constitutional, government
Church of England, Anglican Church
Protestant
monarch, head
Supreme Governor of the Church of England
Archbishop of Canterbury
spiritual
committee
bishop
Presbyterian Church of Scotland
representative, Moderator, Annual General Assembly
Baptists, Presbyterians, Methodists, Quakers
patron saint, holy
feast day
public holiday, Bank Holiday
national holiday, religious holiday

Customs & Traditions

festival
celebrate, celebration
Christmas, Easter, New Year
Eid ul-Fitr, Diwali, Hanukkah
New Year's Eve, Hogmanay
Valentine's day, anonymous, admire
Mother's Day, appreciation
April Fool's day, deceive
Jesus Christ, Good Friday, Easter Sunday
Easter egg
Halloween, ancient, 'trick or treat'
Guy Fawkes Night

bonfire, fireworks
effigy
treason
remembrance
Father Christmas, Santa Claus, Boxing Day

Sport

rugby, cricket
fanatic
Grand National, FA Cup Final, Open championship, Wimbledon

Notting Hill Carnival, London

PRACTICE QUESTIONS

Now test your knowledge of the UK today with these practice questions. Make sure you can answer them all before you take your test.

1. **What is the UK's current population to the nearest million?**

   A 58 million
   B 59 million
   C 60 million
   D 61 million

2. **What percentage of the UK's population lives in Wales?**

   A 8 per cent
   B 84 per cent
   C 5 per cent
   D 3 per cent

3. **What's the name of the survey that collects information about the UK's population?**

   A The Governmental Survey
   B The Official UK Population Register
   C The National Household Survey
   D The Census

4. **How many people live in Scotland?**

   A 3.7 million
   B 5.1 million
   C 10.3 million
   D 8.5 million

5. **Britain's birth rate is falling while its death rate is rising. True or false?**

6. **The population has grown by 7.7 per cent since which year?**

   A 1971
   B 1950
   C 1983
   D 1962

7. **There are more adults aged over 60 than there are children under 16. True or false?**

8. The first official count of the UK's population was taken in 1901. True or false?

9. How often does Britain's census take place?

    A Every year
    B Every century (every 100 years)
    C Every 50 years
    D Every decade (every 10 years)

10. What percentage of the UK population comprises people of Indian, Pakistani, Chinese, Black Caribbean, Black African, Bangladeshi and mixed ethnic backgrounds?

    A 15.4 per cent
    B 8.3 per cent
    C 22.7 per cent
    D 12.1 per cent

11. The public can access the information from the public census ten years after it's gathered. True or false?

12. Since which year have large numbers of people been coming to the UK from Eastern European member states of the EU?

    A 2004
    B 1997
    C 2000
    D 1991

13. How many people of Bangladeshi origin are there living in the UK?

    A 1.3 million
    B 0.3 million
    C 0.7 million
    D 0.2 million

14. Which ethnic group makes up 1.8 per cent of the UK population?

    A Black African
    B Other Asian
    C Indian
    D Chinese

15. More than 90 per cent of Britain's population is white? True or false?

16. **What percentage of the UK's ethnic minority population lives in London?**

   A   53 per cent
   B   45 per cent
   C   37 per cent
   D   28 per cent

17. **A quarter of the population of Greater London comprises people from ethnic minorities. True or false?**

18. **Which UK country is home to less than 1 per cent of the ethnic minority population?**

   A   Wales
   B   Northern Ireland
   C   Scotland
   D   England

19. **What is the longest distance you can travel on the UK mainland?**

   A   427 miles
   B   1,114 miles
   C   870 miles
   D   673 miles

20. **The most northerly place on the British mainland is called Land's End. True or false?**

21. **In which UK city do the locals speak Scouse?**

   A   London
   B   Liverpool
   C   Birmingham
   D   Newcastle

22. **In which two countries are variations of the language Gaelic spoken? Give two answers.**

   A   Wales
   B   Scotland
   C   England
   D   Northern Ireland

23. In some parts of Scotland, people speak an old language called Scots. True or false?

24. In the 2001 census, what percentage of Britain's population said that they had a religion?

   A   75 per cent
   B   99 per cent
   C   67 per cent
   D   83 per cent

25. What percentage of those people with a religion are Christian?

   A   40 per cent
   B   70 per cent
   C   90 per cent
   D   85 per cent

26. People in Scotland and Northern Ireland are less likely to attend a religious service than people in England and Wales. True or false?

27. What percentage of the UK population attends religious services?

   A   57 per cent
   B   69 per cent
   C   35 per cent
   D   10 per cent

28. What percentage of the UK population is Muslim?

   A   5.6 per cent
   B   0.3 per cent
   C   2.7 per cent
   D   1.3 per cent

29. A fifth of British Christians are Roman Catholics. True or false?

30. Roughly what percentage of the UK population says that they have 'no religion'?

   A   5 per cent
   B   10 per cent
   C   15 per cent
   D   20 per cent

31. **What is the name of Britain's official church? Give two answers.**

   A   The Church of Great Britain
   B   The Church of England
   C   The Anglican Church
   D   The English Church

32. **Who is the spiritual leader of the Church of England?**

   A   The Pope
   B   The Archbishop of York
   C   The Archbishop of Canterbury
   D   The Queen

33. **Britain's monarch isn't allowed to marry a Catholic. True or false?**

34. **Which of the following is the established church in Scotland?**

   A   The Scottish Methodists
   B   The Church of Scotland
   C   The Church of England
   D   The Presbyterian Church of Scotland

35. **On which date does Scotland celebrate St Andrew's Day?**

   A   1st March
   B   23rd April
   C   30th November
   D   25th December

36. **Who is the patron saint of Wales?**

   A   St David
   B   St Patrick
   C   St John
   D   St George

37. **The Northern Irish get a day off work on 17th March. True or false?**

38. **How many public holidays are there in England each year?**

   A   10
   B   8
   C   12
   D   6

39. St. George is the patron saint of Britain. True or false?

40. A major arts festival takes place in the Scottish city of Glasgow each year. True or false?

41. On which date is Christmas Day?

   A   1st December
   B   24th December
   C   25th December
   D   26th December

42. Christian children are taught about Muslim religious festivals at school. True or false?

43. What other name do the Scots call New Year's Eve?

   A   Year's End
   B   Hogmanay
   C   Hogshead
   D   Burns Night

44. The Scots get two days off work at New Year. True or false?

45. Who celebrates Valentine's Day on 14th February?

   A   Mothers
   B   Fathers
   C   Lovers
   D   Brothers

46. What does Santa Claus do on Christmas Eve?

   A   Reunite lovers
   B   Scare children
   C   Deliver Easter eggs
   D   Bring presents

47. When is Mother's Day?

   A   A week after Easter
   B   A month before Christmas
   C   Three weeks before Easter
   D   Two months after New Year's Day

48. It's OK for newspapers to print false stories on 1st April. True or false?

49. Which of the following are important Christian festivals? Give two answers.

   A   Easter
   B   Valentine's Day
   C   Christmas
   D   New Year

50. What do British children do on 31st October?

   A   Eat chocolate eggs
   B   Decorate a tree
   C   Buy a gift for their mother
   D   Play tricks on the neighbours

51. Which historical character is 'burned' on a bonfire on 5th November?

   A   Shakespeare
   B   Guy Fawkes
   C   King Henry VIII
   D   Charles Dickens

52. At what time on Remembrance Day is there a two-minute silence?

   A   9am
   B   11am
   C   1pm
   D   11pm

53. On Remembrance Day, people remember those who died fighting in the Second World War. True or false?

54. Which flowers are worn up to and on Remembrance Day?

   A   Daffodils
   B   Roses
   C   Shamrocks
   D   Poppies

55. Christmas celebrates the death and resurrection of Jesus Christ. True or false?

56. What do British people traditionally eat on Christmas Day?

    A   Turkey
    B   Beef
    C   Chocolate
    D   Eggs

57. Father Christmas has a white suit and a red beard. True or false?

58. Which of the following sports do British people like to watch and play? Give two answers.

    A   Football
    B   Baseball
    C   Cricket
    D   Hockey

59. The FA Cup final is a major sporting event in the UK. What does the 'FA' stand for?

    A   Fencing Associates
    B   Football Association
    C   Famous Athletes
    D   Football Aces

60. Britain has four national football teams? True or false?

The answers are on page 203.

Cattistock Hunt, Dorset

Houses of Parliament, London

4.
HOW IS THE UK GOVERNED?

This chapter is about the way the UK is governed or controlled. It examines the monarchy, the political system, the different political parties and the way they're voted into power – as well as the separate administrations in Scotland, Wales and Northern Ireland. It also looks at who can vote and how the public can get involved with politics, and, finally, at Britain's position in Europe and the world.

THE BRITISH CONSTITUTION

Britain is a constitutional democracy. This means that the public holds the power and elects its leaders, who run the country according to a set of rules. A wide range of institutions govern the UK, which ensures that no one organisation has too much power, including:

♦ the monarchy

♦ Parliament (the House of Commons and the House of Lords)

♦ the Prime Minister's office

♦ the Cabinet

♦ the judiciary

♦ the police

♦ the civil service

♦ local government

♂ That Britain is a constitutional democracy with an unwritten constitution.

♂ The different institutions which form the constitution.

In addition, Scotland, Wales and Northern Ireland have their own administrations, which provide some of the direction for these regions. All of the above, together with laws and conventions (or accepted rules), form the British Constitution. Some people also believe that the media (newspapers and television) and pressure groups are also part of the constitution – the law that determines the fundamental political principles of a government.

In many countries, such as America and France, this system is set down in a document, but the British constitution has never been written, partly because the country has never been through a revolution. It has a long, stable and well-established history –

many UK institutions have been in place for hundreds of years. Some people think that Britain should have a written constitution, while others believe that its current form makes it more flexible and able to adapt to change.

The Monarchy

Britain has no president; instead, the country is represented by a monarch (king or queen), who is the head of state. Queen Elizabeth II (2nd) is the Head of State of the United Kingdom, and also of many countries in the Commonwealth. She doesn't rule the country but officially appoints the government, which is chosen by the people in democratic elections. The Queen can advise, warn or encourage the Prime Minister, but decisions regarding government policy can only be made by the Prime Minister and his Cabinet, not by the Queen. This is known as a constitutional monarchy; Spain, the Netherlands, Denmark, Norway and Sweden have similar systems.

The monarch and his or her relatives are called the royal family. The most important members of the British royal family are:

- The Queen – Queen Elizabeth II has reigned since her father died in 1952.

- Prince Charles, the Prince of Wales – As the Queen's eldest son, Prince Charles is heir to the throne, which means he will become the next monarch.

must know

- The UK's head of state is Queen Elizabeth II, but she doesn't rule Britain.

- The Queen can advise, warn or encourage the Prime Minister, but cannot make laws or decisions on government policies.

- The Queen has reigned since 1952 and the heir to the throne is her eldest son, Prince Charles.

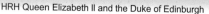

HRH Queen Elizabeth II and the Duke of Edinburgh

Windsor Castle

The Queen represents Britain at home and abroad and is one of the most recognisable images of the country. She has a lot of ceremonial responsibilities, such as opening the new parliamentary session each year, when she makes a speech outlining the government's policies for the coming year.

Government

The UK's governmental system is a parliamentary democracy, which means that the British people vote for representatives to work on their behalf in Parliament – the UK's seat of government. These representatives are called Members of Parliament or MPs.

♦ Each MP represents people in a certain area, called a parliamentary constituency; there are 646 parliamentary constituencies in the UK and the people living there are known as constituents.

♦ MPs are selected by a public vote, known as a general election, which must take place at least every five years. The elected MPs form the House of Commons (see below).

♦ The majority of MPs belong to a political party, and the party with the largest number of MPs is the one that forms the government.

Parliament decides many of the rules of government, although the UK must now accept the rules of the European Union (EU) and the judgements of the European Court, which many believe weakens the power of Parliament.

The House of Commons

The Houses of Parliament are divided into two sections or chambers: the House of Commons and the House of Lords. The House of Commons is more important because its members are elected by the people (as explained above). The Prime Minister and most of the Cabinet – the group of senior ministers in charge of running the Foreign Office, health, defence and other important departments – are members of the Commons.

♦ The members of the House of Commons are called Members of Parliament (MPs).

♦ There is one MP representing each parliamentary constituency or area of the UK; a total of 646.

♦ MPs have a number of different jobs. They represent the people in their constituency, debate important national issues, scrutinise (examine carefully) what the government is doing and help create new laws

Elections

General elections to elect MPs must be held at least every five years, although the Prime Minister can decide to call an earlier election. If, however, an MP dies or resigns between general elections, then a 'by-election' is held in their constituency so that a new MP can be elected.

The UK's election system is called 'first past the post' which means that in each constituency, the candidate who gets the most votes becomes the MP. The government is formed by the political party which has the most MPs.

The five-year rule on elections is a fundamental (basic) law which no government has ever tried to change. In fact, this law is the only one which cannot be changed without the consent (agreement) of the House of Lords.

Whips

The whips are MPs who are chosen by party leaders to maintain order among the party's MPs. They don't actually carry whips, but they do have the power to discipline MPs, and they also make sure that MPs are present in the House of Commons to vote on important issues. The Chief Whip arranges the House of Commons' proceedings with the Speaker of the Houses (an MP from the government party who keeps order) and frequently attends Cabinet and Shadow Cabinet meetings.

European Parliamentary Elections

General elections decide who will represent the people on national matters; European Parliamentary elections decide who will represent the British people in Europe.

♦ Members elected to represent the UK in Europe are called Members of the European Parliament or MEPs. Britain has 78 seats in the European Parliament, therefore there are 78 MEPs.

♦ European Parliamentary elections are held at five-year intervals.

♦ The election system is different from the one used to elect MPs to the British Parliament. Instead, Europe uses 'proportional representation', which means that seats in the European Parliament are allocated to each party in proportion to the number of votes it has gained, therefore a party which receives 50 per cent of the total votes will get 50 per cent of the seats.

must know
!

↻ That the UK is a parliamentary democracy – and how the system works.

↻ The role of MPs – how they're elected and how many there are in the House of Commons.

↻ Why the House of Commons is more important than the House of Lords.

↻ How often elections are held – and what a 'by-election' is.

↻ The 'first past the post' system which decides the UK's elections – and how it works.

↻ What the whips do.

↻ The difference between MPs and MEPs, and how many representatives the UK has in the European Parliament.

↻ The difference between the UK's 'first past the post' election system and the 'proportional representation' system used to elect MEPs.

The House of Lords

Unlike the MPs in the House of Commons, the members of the House of Lords aren't elected by the public and don't represent the public. Although less important than the House of Commons, the House of Lords is more independent of the government. It can propose new laws or suggest amendments (changes) to current laws, which are then discussed by the House of Commons. It can also refuse to pass a law for which the House of Commons has voted, and this can create problems. In this situation, the House of Commons has the power to overrule (decide against) the House of Lords but in practice this power is rarely used.

♦ The members of the House of Lords are called peers. Some peers – called 'hereditary' peers – have had their title of Lord handed down through their family. Peers may also be senior judges or bishops of the Church of England.

♦ Since 1958, the Prime Minister has had the power to appoint peers for their own lifetime, called Life Peers, who cannot pass their title on to their children.

♦ Many Life Peers have had a distinguished (known for its excellence) career in politics, law or some other profession, and can bring more specialist knowledge to the House of Lords than is available to the House of Commons.

♦ Life Peers can be nominated (suggested) by the Prime Minister, the leaders of the other main parties and by an Independent Appointments Commission for non-party peers. They are then appointed by the Queen on the advice of the Prime Minister.

♦ 'Hereditary' peers used to have an automatic right to attend the House of Lords, but in recent years they have lost this right. However, they are allowed to elect some of their own number to represent them.

must know

- The main differences between the House of Commons and the House of Lords – what their powers are and which is more important.

- The difference between a 'hereditary' peer and a Life Peer.

The Prime Minister

The Prime Minister (PM for short) is the most powerful man or woman in the UK government. He or she is the leader of the political party in power (the party which wins the most seats/ constituencies in the general election). The PM is in charge of appointing the Cabinet (see below) and also has control over many important public appointments.

The official residence (home) of the Prime Minister is 10 Downing Street in central London, near to the Houses of Parliament; he also has a country house not far from London called Chequers. Both houses belong to the country and not the Prime Minister, and are used for ceremonial events, such as greeting and entertaining leaders and politicians from other countries.

The Prime Minister may lose his or her job if the MPs in the governing party decide to change their leader. He or she may also resign (step down), which happens when the PM's party is defeated in a general election.

The Cabinet

This is the name of the committee (group) of senior officials who are appointed by the Prime Minister to run the different government departments. There are around 20 members of the Cabinet (it varies), each responsible for a different department, who are usually senior MPs. Some of the different positions and their responsibilities are listed below:

Title	Responsibility
The Chancellor of the Exchequer	Economy
The Foreign Secretary	Relationships with other countries
The Home Secretary	Law, order and immigration
Lord Chancellor	Legal affairs
Secretaries of State	the heads of government departments such as education, health and defence

The Lord Chancellor used to sit in the House of Lords rather than the House of Commons, but a new law was passed in 2005, allowing the Lord Chancellor to sit in the Commons.

The Cabinet meets weekly to make decisions about government policy, which are then debated and approved (or disapproved) by Parliament.

must know

- The role of the Prime Minister – what the job involves and how he or she might lose that job.

- The official residences of the Prime Minister.

- The role of the Cabinet and who is in it – the members' job titles and responsibilities.

The Opposition

The second-largest political party in the House of Commons is called the Opposition – and its main role is to oppose (act against) the government. The Opposition works like a mirror of the governing party. The Leader of the Opposition forms a Shadow Cabinet of senior Opposition MPs who lead criticism of the government, pointing out its failures and weaknesses. An important opportunity to do this occurs each week at Prime Minister's Questions, when the debate can become rather heated.

If his or her party goes on to win the next general election, the Leader of the Opposition becomes the Prime Minister – and faces questions from the new Opposition.

The Speaker

The Speaker is the chief officer and chair of the House of Commons, whose job is to keep order during political debates and ensure that MPs obey the rules. This includes making sure that the Opposition has a guaranteed amount of time in which to debate its chosen issues. The Speaker is an MP who is elected to the position by fellow MPs. However, he or she must remain politically neutral, i.e. not favour or give preferential treatment to any political party.

It's also a ceremonial role as the Speaker represents Parliament at state occasions.

Party System

There are three main political parties in the UK:

♦ The Labour Party (or New Labour).

♦ The Conservatives (also called the Tories).

♦ The Liberal Democrats (also called the Lib Dems).

In addition, there are parties representing the interests of people in Scotland, Wales and Northern Ireland.

Anyone who is a British citizen can stand for election to become an MP, but if they have been nominated to represent a main political party, they are far more likely to win. The few MPs who don't belong to a party are called 'independents'. Anyone can join a political party – it doesn't mean that you have to become an MP and the parties encourage you to join. Party members campaign to promote their party's candidate at general and local government elections, join in debates and contribute money to the party. Most constituencies have local branches for each of the major parties, which hold annual conferences to discuss policy.

must know

⤵ The jobs of the Opposition, the Leader of the Opposition and the Shadow Cabinet.

⤵ The role of the Speaker – and the fact that he or she must be politically neutral.

Pressure & Lobby Groups

As the name suggests, pressure groups are organisations which put pressure on (or lobby) the government to try to influence its policies. There are a lot of pressure groups in the country and they play an important role in politics, not least because they have a lot of support from the public. Even people who aren't interested in joining a political party may support a pressure group, which may represent an economic interest or views on a particular subject. Some well-known pressure groups include:

♦ The Confederation of British Industry – looks after the interests of employers.

♦ The Consumer's Association – stands up for the rights of consumers (the people who use goods and services).

♦ The various trades unions – represent the workers.

♦ Greenpeace – fights for environmental issues.

♦ Liberty – protects and extends human rights.

The Civil Service

The Civil Service is the management and administration arm of the UK government, whose employees are called civil servants and who carry out government policy. They must be professional and politically neutral and cannot be seen to support any one party. However, although they must follow the government's policies, they can warn ministers if they think a policy is impractical (not useful) or not in the public interest. Before a general election takes place, top civil servants will study the Opposition's policies in case that party wins. If they do, the Civil Service must be ready to carry out a new set of aims and policies.

- The three main political parties in the UK and how people can get involved with them.

- The role of pressure and lobby groups.

- What civil servants do.

Devolved Administrations

In 1997, the UK government began a programme of devolving (handing down) power from central government to Scotland and Wales – these are known as devolved administrations and give people in those countries more control over matters which directly affect them. Since 1999, there has been a Scottish Parliament, a Welsh Assembly and, from time to time, a Northern Ireland Assembly. Note that England doesn't have its own separate administration.

The devolved administrations in Scotland and Wales control many public services. However, central UK government still looks after policy and laws governing issues which concern the whole of Britain such as:

- ◆ defence

- ◆ foreign affairs

- ◆ taxation

- ◆ social security

The method of electing the Scottish Parliament and Welsh Assembly is different from the 'first past the post' system which decides general elections. It's called 'proportional representation' and it ensures that each party gets a number of seats in proportion to the number of votes it receives.

Proportional representation is also used in Northern Ireland and this is to ensure 'power sharing' between the Unionist majority, who are mainly Protestant, and the Irish nationalist minority, who are mostly Catholic. In the past, the two sides have been in conflict with each other. A different form of proportional representation decides elections to the European Parliament.

Make sure you know the difference between the two systems of election. 'First past the post' means that the candidate with the most votes wins the constituency or area for his or her party and becomes the MP. The government is then formed by the political party which gains the most constituencies. This system is used in British Parliamentary (general)

Edinburgh, Scotland

elections. 'Proportional representation' means that seats are assigned to each political party in proportion to the percentage of votes it has won. The Scottish Parliament, Welsh Assembly and European Parliament use systems of proportional representation.

Parliament of Scotland

The Scots campaigned for a long time to have more independence from the UK central government and more direct control over their own affairs, which led to the formation, in 1999, of the Scottish Parliament.

♦ The Scottish Parliament sits in Edinburgh, the capital city of Scotland.

♦ There are 129 Members of the Scottish Parliament (MSPs) who are elected (every four years) by a form of proportional representation, where the Scottish Nationalist Party (SNP) governs as a minority administration (they have the most seats but are not in coalition with another party and therefore don't have an overall majority).

♦ The Scottish Parliament can pass laws for Scotland on civil and criminal law, health, education, planning and the raising of additional taxes.

Welsh Assembly Government

The Welsh Assembly Government (WAG) is also called the National Assembly for Wales:

♦ It's located in Cardiff, the capital city of Wales.

♦ There are 60 Assembly Members (AMs) and elections are held every four years.

♦ The members can speak in either Welsh or English and all publications are in both languages.

♦ The WAG can make decisions and pass laws for Wales about local government, transport, health services, education policy and the environment.

Northern Ireland Assembly

Northern Ireland has had its own parliament for far longer than Wales and Scotland. The Northern Ireland Parliament was established in 1922 when Ireland was divided into Northern and Southern Ireland. However, this parliament was abolished (ended) in 1972 as a result of 'the Troubles' (a long-running bloody conflict between those people loyal to the UK and those supporting Irish independence). The Northern Ireland Assembly was established in 1998 after the end of 'the Troubles'.

♦ The Assembly has 108 members, called Members of the Legislative Assembly (MLAs). Power sharing ensures that ministers are chosen equally from the main political parties.

♦ The MLAs can make decisions about health and social services, the environment, agriculture and education in Northern Ireland.

♦ UK central government has the power to suspend the Northern Ireland Assembly if problems occur; for example, if the political leaders cannot agree to work together or the Assembly isn't serving the interests of the Northern Irish people. This has happened several times, most recently in 2006. When the Assembly is suspended, the MLAs cannot pass bills or make decisions.

must know

⟳ What is a 'devolved administration' and when did the UK government decide to 'devolve' power.

⟳ The names of the three devolved administrations in Scotland, Wales and Northern Ireland – how many members they have and what these members are called.

⟳ The areas of laws and policies which the devolved administrations can decide.
The areas of laws and policies which only UK central government can decide.

⟳ The main difference between the administration in Scotland and Wales, and the one in Northern Ireland.

Local Government

Just as UK central government looks after Britain as a whole, local government authorities take care of local policies and services in every city, town and rural area of the country. They're usually known as local authorities or councils. Some areas have district and county councils which have different functions, but most large towns and cities have a single local authority. London has one main authority, the Greater London Authority (GLA), and a further 33 local authorities.

The mayor may be the leader of the administration, like the Mayor of London who coordinates policy across all the different local authorities, or he or she may just be a ceremonial figurehead. Elections for local councillors are held in May, when anyone from the local community can stand to be a councillor (many do so as members of a national political party).

Local authorities must provide the following 'mandatory' services:

♦ Education

♦ Libraries

♦ Planning

- Refuse collection
- Environmental health
- Fire service
- Passenger transport
- Housing
- Social services

To help you remember these, try learning the phrase *Every Little Penguin Runs Extremely Fast Past Hungry Seals.*

Local authorities spend a lot of money on the above services, most of which is received from central government, with around 20 per cent raised from 'council tax', a local tax which helps to pay for local services, the level of which is set by individual local authorities. It applies to all domestic properties (e.g. houses, flats, bungalows, maisonettes, mobile homes and houseboats) and residents, whether they're owners or tenants, must pay council tax.

Judiciary

This is the name for the judges who interpret (explain) UK law. In Britain, the most important laws are made by Parliament; however, it's the job of judges to decide how to apply them. The government isn't allowed to interfere. On occasion, there are claims that the actions of the government are illegal and judges must decide if this is true; if they agree, then the government must change its policies or ask Parliament to change the law.

- The responsibilities of local councils – *Every Little Penguin Runs Extremely Fast Past Hungry Seals.*
- The role of the councillors and the mayor.
- When local elections are held.
- The proportion of money raised by council tax – and who pays it.

- **The Human Rights Act** – Judges now have the job of applying the Human Rights Act. If they decide that a public body, such as the government, isn't respecting a person's human rights, the judges may order it to change its practices and, if necessary, to pay compensation. The Human Rights Act can even affect Acts of Parliament – laws that have been decided by Parliament. If an Act of Parliament is judged to be incompatible with (doesn't work together with, or contradicts) the Human Rights Act, judges can ask Parliament to change it, even though they cannot change it themselves.

- **The jury system** – Judges cannot decide if an individual is guilty or innocent of a serious crime. A jury, which is a group of 12 members of the general public chosen at random for jury service, makes this important decision, and – if found guilty – the judge then decides on the penalty. In the case of less serious crimes, a magistrate decides whether the accused is guilty or not, and what the penalty should be.

Police

The police prevent and investigate crime. The police service is locally organised, with a service for each county (an administrative area) or group of counties. The largest is the Metropolitan Police (the Met), which serves the Greater London area and is based at New Scotland Yard. The whole of Northern Ireland is served by the Police Service for Northern Ireland (PSNI).

The police have 'operational independence', which means that the government cannot tell them what to do in any particular case. However, their independence is limited, as their finances are controlled by the government and by police authorities who consist of councillors and magistrates. In addition, their powers are limited by the law. If somebody makes a serious complaint against the police, it's investigated by the Independent Police Complaints Commission (IPCC) – or, in Northern Ireland, by the Police Ombudsman.

must know

- ⟳ Parliament makes the laws in the UK but the judiciary interprets them.
- ⟳ Judges' involvement in the Human Rights Act.
- ⟳ Who can decide guilt or innocence in a serious – and not so serious – crime.
- ⟳ How the police are structured and organised – and who deals with complaints against them.
- ⟳ What quangos are and what do they do.

Non-departmental Public Bodies (QUANGOS)

Quango stands for QUAsi Non-GOvernmental Organisation – also called non-departmental public bodies – to which the government has given power. They carry out work on behalf of the public which it would be inappropriate (wrong) to place under the control of a Cabinet minister. Although ministers can appoint staff to these bodies, they must do so in a fair and open way. There are many hundreds of quangos in the UK, carrying out a wide range of duties.

The Role of the Media

Events in Parliament are made available to the public through a variety of media: proceedings are broadcast on digital television and published in official reports, such as Hansard. Hansard is available on the internet (🖥 www.parliament.uk) and in main libraries.

However, most people find out about governmental issues through the press, which consists primarily of newspapers, television, radio and, more recently, the internet. The UK has a free press, meaning that what is written in newspapers or broadcast on other media is free from government control. In fact, the editors and owners of newspapers tend to have strong political opinions, and express them in their stories and in campaigns where they try to influence government policy and public opinion. As a result, it's sometimes difficult to tell facts from opinion in newspaper reporting.

In theory, there is more control in the run up to elections when the law requires radio and television coverage to be balanced; this means that equal time is given to all rival viewpoints, although broadcasters are still free to interview politicians in a hard-hitting and lively way.

Who Can Vote?

The UK has a fully democratic system. This has been in place since 1928, when women were given the right to vote at 21, the same age as men. The voting age was reduced to 18 in 1969. All UK-born and naturalised citizens have the right and duty to vote, and to do jury service (see above), with few exceptions; for example, convicted prisoners cannot vote.

All UK citizens, as well as citizens of the Commonwealth and the Irish Republic can also vote in all public elections, but only if they're resident in the UK. Citizens of EU states who are resident in the UK can vote in all elections except national parliamentary (general) elections.

- How Parliament makes its proceedings available to the public.

- Which elements constitute the UK press.

- What is meant by a 'free press' – and how some newspapers interpret this.

The Electoral Register

This is the register, or list, of all the people who are eligible (qualified) to vote. If you want to vote in a general, local or European election, you must have your name on the electoral register.

◆ In England, Scotland and Wales, you can register (add your name) by contacting your local council election registration office. If you don't know who your local authority is, contact the Local Government Association's (LGA) information line (☎ 020-7664 3131, 6am to 5pm Monday to Friday). Tell them your postcode or full address and they will give you the name of your local authority. You can also obtain voter registration forms in English, Welsh and some other languages via the internet (🖥 www.electoralcommission.org.uk). The electoral register is updated each year in September or October. A form is sent to every household and must be completed and returned with the names of everyone who's living in the house and eligible to vote on October 15 of that year.

◆ In Northern Ireland, the electoral registration system is different, as it collects registration details from individuals rather than households. Everyone who's entitled to vote must complete their own registration form. Once you're registered you stay on the register as long as your personal details don't change – there's no annual electoral register form to complete. For more information, contact the Electoral Office for Northern Ireland (☎ 028-9044 6688).

Anyone can examine the electoral register, although this must be supervised. The register is kept at each local electoral registration office (or council office in England and Wales). Some libraries also keep a copy of the register.

Standing for Office

Some people want to become Members of Parliament, a member of one of the devolved administrations or a local councillor, which is called standing for public office. Most citizens of the UK, the Irish Republic or the Commonwealth, who are aged 18 or over, may stand for public office. Those who cannot include civil servants, members of the armed forces and those found guilty of certain crimes. Members of the House of Lords cannot stand for election as MPs to the House of Commons, although they are allowed to stand for other public offices.

If you want to stand as a councillor in a local authority, you must have a connection to the council area. This may include:

♦ having your name on the electoral register;

♦ working locally;

♦ owning or renting land or property in the area.

must know

↻ When women received the right to vote at the same age as men.

↻ The current minimum voting age in the UK – and in what year this age was set.

↻ The rights and duties of UK citizens. Who can vote in UK elections – and who cannot.

↻ How and when you can register to vote.

↻ Where the electoral register is kept.

↻ The basic requirements for standing for public office – as a member or a councillor.

Contacting Elected Members

All elected members have a duty to serve and represent their constituents. In other words, MPs and councillors work for you, therefore it's important that you're able to contact them. There are several ways to do this:

♦ **At the library**: Contact details for all your representatives and their political parties are available at your local library.

♦ **In the phone book**: MPs, MEPs, MSPs and Assembly members are listed in the phone book and the Yellow Pages (a business directory sent to each household).

♦ **At their office**: MPs can be contacted by letter or phone at their constituency office.

♦ **At the House of Commons**: MPs can be contacted by letter or phone at the House of Commons (House of Commons, Westminster, London SW1A 0AA, ☎ 020-7729 3000).

♦ **By fax**: You can find out the name of your local MP and contact them by fax through the website 🖥 www.writetothem.com. This service is free.

♦ **In person**: Many MPs, MEPs, MSPs and Assembly members hold 'surgeries' in their constituencies, where people can discuss issues or problems. Surgeries are advertised in local newspapers.

How to Visit Parliament & the Devolved Administrations

The public is free to visit the Houses of Parliament and the administrations in Scotland, Wales and Northern Ireland, to tour the buildings and to watch debates. Here's how to arrange a visit:

The Houses of Parliament

You can listen to debates in the Palace of Westminster from the public galleries in both the House of Commons and the House of Lords. Tickets are free. It's possible to queue on the day, although it can take up to two hours to get into the House of Commons – it's easier to visit the House of Lords. Alternatively, write to your MP in advance and ask for tickets. For more information, see the UK Parliament website (🖳 www.parliament. uk).

The Scottish Parliament

Members of the Scottish Parliament (MSPs) meet at Holyrood in Edinburgh (🖳 www. scottish.parliament.uk). You can obtain information, book tickets and arrange tours through visitor services: Scottish Parliament, Edinburgh, EH99 1SP (☎ 0131-348 5200).

The Welsh Assembly

The elected members (AMs) meet in the Welsh Assembly in the Senedd in Cardiff Bay (🖳 www.wales.gov.uk). To book seats in the public galleries or a guided tour of the Senedd, contact the Assembly booking line (☎ 029-2089 8477).

The Northern Ireland Assembly

Members of the Legislative Assembly (MLA) meet at Stormont in Belfast. You can arrange a visit to Stormont by contacting your MLA or the Education Service (🖳 www.niassembly.gov.uk).

must know

- ⌁ How to contact elected members and local representatives.

- ⌁ That the public is free to visit the Houses of Parliament and the administrations in Scotland, Wales and Northern Ireland.

- ⌁ How to obtain tickets for the Houses of Parliament.

- ⌁ How to visit the devolved administrations in Scotland, Wales and Northern Ireland.

- ⌁ The basic requirements for standing for public office – as a member or a councillor.

Welsh Assembly building (Senedd), Cardiff

THE UK: EUROPE & THE WORLD

The Commonwealth

The United Kingdom has a unique place in the Commonwealth, which is an association of 53 nations. Many member countries were originally a part of the British Empire (those countries which were once governed by Britain), but a few extra countries have also joined.

The main aims of the Commonwealth are to promote democracy and good government and to eradicate (end) poverty. The Queen is the head of the Commonwealth, although this is a symbolic role – she has no power over the member states. The Commonwealth itself has no power over its members, although it can suspend membership if a country fails to uphold its ideals.

The 53 members of the Commonwealth are:

Antigua and Barbuda	Kenya	Samoa
Australia	Kiribati	Seychelles
The Bahamas	Lesotho	Sierra Leone
Bangladesh	Malawi	Singapore
Barbados	Malaysia	Solomon Islands
Belize	Maldives	South Africa
Botswana	Malta	Sri Lanka
Brunei Darussalam	Mauritius	Swaziland
Cameroon	Mozambique	Tonga
Canada	Namibia	Trinidad and Tobago
Cyprus	Nauru (special	Tuvalu
Dominica	member)	Uganda
Fiji Islands	New Zealand	United Kingdom
The Gambia	Nigeria	United Republic of
Ghana	Pakistan	Tanzania
Grenada	Papua New Guinea	Vanuatu
Guyana	St Kitts and Nevis	Zambia
India	St Lucia	
Jamaica	St Vincent and the	
	Grenadines	

must know

- There are 53 member states in the Commonwealth, including the UK.
- The aims and powers of the Commonwealth.
- The role of the Queen.

The European Union

The European Union (EU) was founded on 25th March 1957, when it was called the European Economic Community (EEC) and was made up of the six countries which signed the Treaty of Rome: Belgium, France, Germany, Italy, Luxembourg and the Netherlands. The idea behind the treaty (agreement) and the new community was to encourage cooperation between Europe's states and reduce the likelihood of another war.

The UK wasn't one of the founder (original) members and it only joined the EU in 1973, 16 years after it was established, but has since become an important member. An additional ten countries joined in 2004, followed by two more in 2007. The EU currently has 27 members.

Important points to know about Britain and the EU include the following:

♦ **The Euro** – The EU is aiming for its member states to function as a single market with a single shared currency, the Euro. Many EU countries now use the Euro, but Britain has decided to retain its own currency unless the British people vote in a referendum (a vote to decide an issue) to accept the Euro – which they currently appear unlikely to do!

♦ **Free movement** – Citizens of an EU state have the right to travel and work in any EU country, provided they have a valid passport or identity card, which has led to many Eastern Europeans migrating to the UK. However, these rights can be restricted on the grounds of public health, public order and public security. For citizens of countries which have joined the EU more recently, the right to work is also sometimes restricted for a number of years.

♦ **The Council of the European Union** – This is the governing body of the EU, comprised of ministers from all the EU countries – for this reason, it's usually called **The Council of Ministers**. Together with the European Parliament, it's the legislative body of the EU, which makes, amends and repeals laws. The Council of Ministers passes EU law, acting on recommendations from the European Commission and the European Parliament, and makes the most important decisions about how the EU is run.

♦ **The European Commission** – This is the civil service of the EU. It drafts proposals (makes suggestions) for new EU policies and administers its funding programmes. The European Commission is based in Brussels, the capital of Belgium.

♦ **The European Parliament** – This is the only directly elected institution in the EU. Members of the European Parliament, or MEPs, are elected to represent their country in elections every five years. The European Parliament examines decisions made by the European Commission and the European Council, which is formed by the heads of state of the member countries. It can refuse to agree to laws proposed by the Commission and can also monitor how EU money is being spent. It meets in Strasbourg, in north-eastern France, and also in Brussels.

♦ **European Union law** – All the EU member states, including the UK, have to obey EU law. European laws are called directives, regulations or framework decisions, and they've had a big effect on people's rights in the UK, especially at work. There are European directives about making people redundant (laying them off from their job), as well as regulations which limit the number of hours people can be made to work.

The Council of Europe

The Council of Europe is completely separate from the European Union. It was created in 1949, eight years before the EU was formed, and has a different purpose. The UK is one of the founder members of the Council, and most other European countries have joined.

The Council of Europe doesn't make laws. Instead, it draws up charters and conventions (agreements) which focus on human rights, democracy, education, the environment, health and culture. The most important is the European Convention on Human Rights Act of 1998, which defines the 16 basic rights which all people should have. All the member states must obey this convention and those which don't risk being expelled (removed) from the Council.

Don't confuse the Council of Europe with the Council of the European Union. The Council of Europe is a separate and older organisation and has no role within the EU. The Council of the European Union is the organisation which governs the EU and passes its laws.

must know

- When the European Union was first founded – and why.
- When the UK joined the EU.
- The number of countries which make up the current EU.
- Britain's position on the Euro.
- The rights of people from EU member states to travel and work in Europe.
- What the Council of Ministers is and what it does.
- What the European Commission is and what it does.
- The role of the European Parliament and how often its members are elected.
- Where the European Commission and the European Parliament meet.
- The effects European Union law has on UK workers.

The United Nations (UN)

The United Nations (UN) is an international organisation that was established just after the Second World War with the aim of promoting international peace and security and preventing further wars. UN peacekeepers (with blue berets) are a familiar sight on television in areas of conflict around the world.

Over 190 countries belong to the UN and the UK is one of the 15 members of the UN Security Council, which recommends action by the UN when there's an international crisis or threat to world peace. It's also one of the five permanent members of the council, along with China, France, Russia and the USA.

The UN has produced three important agreements affecting the rights of people, women and children:

◆ The Universal Declaration of Human Rights

◆ The Convention on the Elimination of All Forms of Discrimination against Women

◆ The UN Convention on the Rights of the Child

None of these are laws, but they are widely used in legal cases and in political debate in order to reinforce (strengthen) the law and to assess the behaviour of countries.

- The difference between the Council of Europe and the Council of the European Union.
- The history and role of the Council of Europe.
- The importance of the European Convention on Human Rights.
- The function of the United Nations – and how many nations make up the UN.
- Britain's role within the UN.
- The UN's most important agreements.

WORDS TO LEARN

Check that you understand this chapter's key terms:

The British Constitution

constitution, institution
democracy
convention
revolution
monarchy, monarch, constitutional
monarchy
rule, reign, heir
ceremonial
parliament, parliamentary democracy
Member of Parliament
House of Commons, House of Lords
constituency, constituent
elect, general election, by-election
debate, scrutinise
first past the post, proportional
representation
fundamental
consent
whip
amendment, overrule
hereditary peer, life peer
nominate, appoint
residence
resign
cabinet, committee
esponsibility

economy
opposition, oppose
Speaker, neutral
political party, independent, campaign
pressure group, lobby
civil servant, administration
devolve, devolved administration
policy
power sharing
abolish
local authority, council, councillor
mayor
planning
refuse (garbage) collection
the environment, environmental health
social services
funding, council tax
domestic property
judiciary, judge
compensation, incompatible
Act of Parliament
jury, magistrate
police service, investigate
quango, non-departmental public body
Hansard
media, press, free press
opinion

vote, voter
electoral register, eligible, household
standing for public office
Holyrood, the Senedd, Stormont

The UK in Europe and the World

Commonwealth
symbolic
eradicate
European Union
treaty, community
single market, shared currency

referendum
free movement
legislative, amend, repeal
draft, proposal, funding
directive, regulation, framework decision
redundant
charter, convention
human rights, Human Rights Act
expel
United Nations
conflict, reinforce

PRACTICE QUESTIONS

Now test your knowledge of how the UK is governed with these practice questions. Make sure that you can answer them all before you take your test.

1.   **What sort of governmental system does the UK have?**

    A   Communist
    B   Constitutional democracy
    C   Tyranny
    D   Labour

2.   **The British Constitution is a written constitution. True or false?**

3.   **The House of Lords and House of Commons together form which UK institution?**

    A   10 Downing Street
    B   The Parliament of Scotland
    C   The UK Parliament
    D   The Northern Ireland Assembly

4.   **Who is the head of state for the UK and the Commonwealth?**

    A   Prince Charles
    B   Queen Elizabeth II
    C   The Prime Minister
    D   President George W Bush

5.   **Who makes decisions about the UK government?**

    A   The Prime Minister
    B   The Queen
    C   The Prime Minister and the Queen
    D   The Prime Minister and the Cabinet

6.   **Which of these statements is correct?**

    A   The Queen can advise, order and rule the Prime Minister
    B   The Queen can advise, warn and encourage the Prime Minister

7. **When did the reign of Queen Elizabeth II begin?**

    A   1982
    B   1952
    C   1957
    D   1962

8. **How many parliamentary constituencies are there?**

    A   646
    B   876
    C   537
    D   621

9. **Which parliamentary chamber is most important?**

    A   They are equally important
    B   The House of Lords
    C   The House of Commons
    D   10 Downing Street

10. **General elections must take place at least every five years. True or false?**

11. **Where are MPs elected to?**

    A   The House of Lords
    B   The Labour Party
    C   The Cabinet
    D   The House of Commons

12. **UK parliamentary elections are decided by proportional representation. True or false?**

13. **In a party, who is responsible for attendance and discipline among its MPs?**

    A   The party leader
    B   The party whips
    C   The party chains
    D   The secretary

14. **How many seats does the UK have in the European Parliament?**

    A   78
    B   87
    C   96
    D   68

15. **Which of these statements is true?**

A   MPs can represent their constituents in the European Parliament.
B   Constituents are represented in the European Parliament by MEPs.

16. **Since when has the Prime Minister had the power to appoint peers for their lifetime?**

A   1987
B   1983
C   1957
D   1958

17. **The House of Lords can pass new laws. True or false?**

18. **What title can a political party's leader sometimes have? Give two answers.**

A   Chief Whip
B   The Prime Minister
C   Shadow Secretary
D   The Leader of the Opposition

19. **Where does the Prime Minister live? Give two answers.**

A   10 Downing Street
B   The Houses of Parliament
C   Buckingham Palace
D   Chequers

20. **What name is given to the group of senior MPs who become departmental ministers?**

A   The Cabinet
B   The Shadow Cabinet
C   The Home Secretaries
D   The Chancellors of the Exchequer

21. **The Lord Chancellor is responsible for the economy. True or false?**

22. **What title is given to the second-largest party in the House of Commons?**

A   The Second Party
B   The Opposition
C   The Rival Party
D   The Adversaries

23. **How many ministers make up the Cabinet?**

    A 5
    B 10
    C 15
    D 20

24. **Which of the following statements is true?**

    A The Speaker is the chief officer of the House of Commons and is voted in by the MPs.
    B The Speaker is the chief officer of the House of Lords and is chosen by the Queen.

25. **Which party does the Speaker represent?**

    A The largest party in the House of Commons
    B The second-largest party in the House of Commons
    C None, he or she is politically neutral
    D All the independent MPs

26. **Which of the following political parties are represented in the House of Commons? Give two answers.**

    A The Conservatives
    B The Democrats
    C The Conservationists
    D The Liberal Democrats

27. **How often do parties hold policy-making conferences?**

    A Annually
    B Every six months
    C Monthly
    D Every five years

28. **A member of the general public is more likely to do what than join a political party?**

    A Vote
    B Stand for office
    C Support a pressure group
    D Visit the House of Commons

29. **Civil servants, who carry out government policy, mustn't support a particular political party. True or false?**

30. **When did the government begin a programme of devolving power from the central government?**

    A   1999
    B   1995
    C   1992
    D   1997

31. **Name the area of government which the devolved administrations cannot control.**

    A   Health
    B   The Environment
    C   Agriculture
    D   Defence

32. **How many AMs are there in the Welsh Assembly Government?**

    A   60
    B   108
    C   129
    D   75

33. **Which of the following is the odd one out?**

    A   The Parliament of Scotland
    B   The National Assembly for Wales
    C   The Northern Ireland Assembly
    D   The English Parliament

34. **Who has the power to suspend The Northern Ireland Assembly?**

    A   The Foreign Minister
    B   The UK government
    C   The Queen
    D   The MLAs (Members of the Legislative Assembly)

35. **What does the proportional representation electoral system mean in practice?**

    A   The party which puts forward the most candidates wins.
    B   The party which gains the largest share of the votes wins.
    C   The party which gains the most constituencies wins.
    D   All the parties share power equally.

36. **Which of the following are 'mandatory' services provided by local councils? Give two answers.**

    A   Doctor's surgeries
    B   Shopping centres
    C   Libraries
    D   Refuse collection

37. **People who live in mobile homes don't have to pay council tax. True or false?**

38. **Which of the following two statements is correct?**

    A   Local authorities receive 20 per cent of their funding from the government and 80 per cent from council tax.
    B   The government funds 80 per cent of local authority spending and the rest is raised by council tax.

39. **Whose job is it to interpret the law?**

    A   The jury
    B   The police
    C   The judges
    D   The Prime Minister

40. **Who decides if a person is guilty or innocent of a less serious crime?**

    A   A judge
    B   A magistrate
    C   A jury
    D   The police

41. **In certain circumstances, the government can tell the police service what to do. True or false?**

42. **What name is given to non-departmental bodies that act on behalf of the public?**

    A   Quangos
    B   Fangos
    C   Tangos
    D   Kangos

43. **When must television and radio give airtime to the viewpoints of all political parties?**

    A   All the time
    B   At Christmas
    C   In the run-up to elections
    D   Just after elections

44. **Which of the following statements is correct?**

    A   The government cannot tell the owners and editors what to write.
    B   The owners and editors of newspapers cannot write what they like about the government.

45. **In which year were 18-year-olds first allowed to vote?**

    A   1969
    B   1979
    C   1928
    D   1990

46. **Citizens of European Union countries who are living in the UK cannot vote in all elections. True or false?**

47. **During which months is the electoral register updated?**

    A   January and February
    B   March and April
    C   June and July
    D   September and October

48. **What must someone have in order to stand as a councillor?**

    A   A local connection
    B   A successful professional career
    C   A degree
    D   A job in a political field

49. **Where does the Scottish Parliament meet?**

    A   Hollywood
    B   Holyrood
    C   Holyroad
    D   Holyhead

50. **Where is the Senedd?**

    A London
    B Cardiff
    C Edinburgh
    D Belfast

51. **How many member states does the Commonwealth currently have?**

    A 53
    B 43
    C 33
    D 63

52. **Which treaty was signed at the founding of the European Economic Community?**

    A The Treaty of London
    B The Maastricht Treaty
    C The Treaty of Rome
    D The Treaty of Europe

53. **The UK is one of the founding members of the European Union. True or false?**

54. **How many member states are there in the EU?**

    A 24
    B 25
    C 26
    D 27

55. **Which of the European institutions makes and amends the law. Give two answers.**

    A The European Parliament
    B The European Commission
    C The Council of Europe
    D The Council of Ministers

56. **Where does the European Parliament meet? Give two answers.**

    A Brussels
    B London
    C Strasbourg
    D Paris

57. How often are elections held for MEPs?

   A Every four years
   B Annually
   C Every three years
   D Every five years

58. European directives have no direct effect on the lives of UK workers. True or false?

59. Which of the following was drawn up by the Council of Europe?

   A The Universal Declaration of Human Rights
   B The Convention on the Elimination of All Forms of Discrimination against Women
   C The European Convention on Human Rights
   D The Declaration of European Independence

60. How many countries are members of the UN Security Council?

   A 15
   B 190
   C 90
   D 5

The answers are on page 204.

Bodiam Castle, East Sussex

5.

EVERYDAY NEEDS

This chapter explains the things you need to know about day-to-day living in the UK. It covers the different types of accommodation and utility services, such as electricity, water and council services; it looks at money, banking and credit; and provides information about the UK's health and education services. It also examines leisure options, driving and public transport, and explains the kind of identity documents used in Britain.

HOUSING

Housing is the biggest priority for people in Britain, which is a small country with a large population. Accommodation can be expensive. Even so, around two-thirds of people own their own homes, usually with the help of a loan called a mortgage. The remainder rent houses, flats or rooms from local authorities, housing associations or private landlords.

Buying a Home

Most Britons who can afford to buy, do so, as it's generally no more expensive than renting and is generally a good long-term investment.

Mortgages

Housing prices have risen a great deal in the UK and many people are finding it difficult to buy their first home – known as 'getting on the property ladder'. Most buyers will take out a mortgage, a type of loan used to buy a home. This is paid back, with interest, over a long period of time, usually 25 years. Banks and building societies arrange mortgages, and these are the best places to find information. A few banks can help with Islamic (Sharia) mortgages, which avoid charging interest in the standard way, a practice which is unacceptable to Muslims.

Some people have problems making the repayments on their mortgage – and risk losing their home. If this happens to you, it's important that you speak to your lender (bank or building society) as soon as possible. You can also obtain help and advice from government and other authorities.

Estate Agents

Most people sell their homes through estate agents, therefore this is the first place to go if you want to buy a home. Estate agents represent (act for) the person who is selling a property, called the vendor, and arrange for prospective buyers to view (visit) homes that are for sale. There are estate agents in every town and city, most with websites where they advertise homes for sale. You can also find details about homes for sale on general websites and in the property sections of local and national newspapers.

Scotland has a different system and no estate agents; if you want to buy a home you must go to a solicitor (lawyer) first.

Making an Offer

If you decide to buy a home, you first make an offer to the seller based on the amount of money you wish to pay. The process depends on where you are in the UK:

♦ **In England, Wales and Northern Ireland**, you generally do this through the estate agent or a solicitor. Usually, people make offers which are lower than the asking price. Offers are made 'subject to contract', which means that you can withdraw from the deal if there are reasons why you cannot go ahead and complete the purchase.

♦ **In Scotland**, the seller sets a price for their property and buyers make offers above that amount. The buyer who makes the best offer gets the house, and the contract between seller and buyer is legally binding, meaning neither side can back out (this only applies after the exchange of contracts in the rest of the UK).

Solicitor & Surveyor

These professionals are an important part of the process of buying a house or flat.

♦ **Solicitors** handle the legal side of buying a home. When you make an offer, the solicitor will carry out a number of legal checks on the property, the seller and the local area. They will also prepare the legal contract which you will need to buy the property.

♦ **Surveyors** carry out checks on the property you want to buy, to make sure that there are no structural problems, i.e. problems with the structure or build of the house or flat. If you're taking on a mortgage, your lender (bank or building society) will ask a surveyor to make this check. As the buyer doesn't get to see the results of the lender's survey (check), they often ask a second surveyor to examine the property on their behalf.

In Scotland, these checks help buyers decide the price they should offer for the house, therefore the survey often takes place before an offer is made.

must know

- Two-thirds of people in the UK own their homes.
- What mortgages are, how long they are paid for and where to find information.
- Where to find property for sale.
- The roles of estate agents, solicitors and surveyors.
- The important differences between buying property in Scotland and the rest of the UK.

Renting

Not everyone wants or can afford to buy a home. The alternative is to rent, and you can rent accommodation from a local authority (council), from a housing association or from a private property owner, called a landlord.

The Local Authority

Most local government authorities (or councils) provide housing – often called social housing or 'council housing'. Everyone is entitled to apply for housing in their local authority area, which you do by putting your name on the council register or list, which is available from the housing department.

You're assessed on a 'points basis', which means that you get more points according to your needs, e.g. if you're homeless or have children or have chronic (long-term) ill health; and the more points you have, the sooner you will get a home. Note, however, that council housing can be hard to obtain, as there's a shortage of council accommodation and a high demand for it, therefore some people must wait a long time.

♦ In Scotland, information about social housing is available from 💻 www.sfha.co.uk.

♦ In Northern Ireland, social housing is provided by the Northern Ireland Housing Executive (💻 www.nihe.co.uk).

Housing Associations

Housing associations are independent not-for-profit organisations which provide housing for rent. They work separately from lenders and don't aim to make money out of people looking for a home, and offer affordable housing – in some areas they also manage local authority (council) accommodation. Housing associations mainly manage rental property, but they also help people buy their own homes by operating schemes that allow people to buy part of a house or flat if they can't afford to buy it all in one go. Schemes like this are referred to as 'shared ownership'.

Private Rented Accommodation

A lot of people rent their house or flat from a private landlord. You can find information about private rented accommodation in local newspapers, on the internet, and on notice boards in shops and supermarkets. There are also estate agents who deal with rented property, called letting agents.

Tenancy Agreement

When you move into a privately rented property you sign a tenancy agreement or lease, which sets out the conditions or 'rules' that you must follow as the tenant (the person who rents), e.g. some landlords don't allow you to keep pets. Always check this agreement carefully to avoid any problems or misunderstandings later on. The agreement also contains an inventory which is a list of any furniture and fittings, e.g. kitchen cupboards and light fittings, in the property.

Before signing the agreement, you must check the details, and make sure that all the items are present in the property and check their condition. If any items are found to be missing or damaged at the end of the tenancy – the period of time you're renting for – you may be charged for it or money may be deducted from your deposit (see below).

Deposit & Rent

You fix the rent with the landlord at the beginning of the tenancy and it cannot be increased without your agreement. Most landlords also ask for a deposit, which is a sum of money paid to cover the cost of any damage, usually equal to one month's rent. The landlord must return this money to you at the end of the tenancy, unless you have caused damage. Both the rent and the deposit must be stated in the tenancy agreement.

If you have a low income or are unemployed, you may be able to claim housing benefit to help pay your rent.

Ending & Renewing a Tenancy

Tenancy agreements last for a fixed period, usually six months. You then have the option of ending the tenancy and moving out, or renewing (starting again from new) the tenancy with the agreement of the landlord. If you leave a property before the end of the tenancy, you will probably have to pay rent for the rest of the term that you agreed to rent the property, unless you can find someone else to take over the lease.

A landlord cannot force a tenant to leave before the tenancy is over. There are procedures that landlords must follow if they want a tenant to leave, which depend on the type of tenancy. It's against the law (a criminal offence) for a landlord to use threats or violence against a tenant to leave, and he must have a court order (a ruling from a court) to force a tenant to leave before the lease expires.

Discrimination

Landlords must not discriminate against a tenant looking for somewhere to live because of their nationality, race, sex, or ethnic group, or because they are disabled. The only situation where they can do this is if the landlord or a close relative will be sharing the accommodation with the tenant.

Homelessness

There's a problem with homelessness in the UK, where some people live on the streets. If you have no home or place to stay, you should ask for help from your local authority (or, in Northern Ireland, the Housing Executive). They have a legal duty to offer help

must know

- ✐ The three main places where you can rent accommodation.
- ✐ What 'points' are and how local authorities decide who is a priority for social housing.
- ✐ That there may be a long waiting list for local authority (council) accommodation.
- ✐ What housing associations do.
- ✐ Where to look for private rented accommodation.
- ✐ What a tenancy agreement, inventory and deposit are.
- ✐ What landlords can and cannot do.

and advice – but they don't have to offer you a place to live. In order for your council to offer you somewhere to live, you must:

- ◆ have a priority need – see **The Local Authority** above;
- ◆ have a connection, e.g. a job or family, in the council's area;
  prove that you haven't made yourself 'intentionally homeless', e.g. by choosing not to pay your mortgage or rent.

Finding Help

The following organisations can help if you have problems with your landlord or become homeless:

- ◆ The **local authority's (council) housing department** – provides advice on homelessness and Housing Benefit (money to help pay your rent). It also deals with problems with local authority housing.
- ◆ The **Citizens' Advice Bureau**, which has offices in most large towns and advises on a range of problems, including housing.
- ◆ **Shelter** – a national housing charity (☎ 0808-800 4444, 🖥 www.shelternet.org.uk).
- ◆ The **Department for Work and Pensions (DWP)** – this government organisation runs the Social Fund. When someone is setting up a home after being homeless or after coming out of prison or another institution, they may be entitled to a Community Care Grant from

the Social Fund. Loans are also available to people who've suffered an emergency, such as flooding. Information about these grants and loans is available from Jobcentre Plus or from a Citizens' Advice Bureau.

must know

Where to get help if you're homeless, have problems with your landlord or cannot pay the rent.

SERVICES FOR THE HOME

These include utilities such as electricity and water, for which you receive bills, as well as services provided by the local authority and paid for in your council tax (such as refuse collection).

Water

All UK homes are supplied with piped water and the charge for this is called water rates. When you move into a new home as a tenant or owner, you should receive a letter from the company that supplies your water, so that you can make arrangements to pay them. Water rates can be paid in a single payment (a lump sum) or in instalments (several smaller payments), usually monthly. The cost depends on the size of your property – larger houses pay more than small flats. Some homes have a water meter, where you pay only for the water you've used.

♦ People who receive Housing Benefit may have their water rates paid by the benefit payment.

♦ In Northern Ireland, water charges are included in the domestic rates (see **Council Tax** on page 108).

Electricity & Gas

All UK properties are supplied with electricity at 240 volts and most homes in towns also have a gas supply (except in rural areas). Both electricity and gas are metered, and when you move into a new home or leave an old one, you should make a note of the electricity and gas meter readings.

Supply Problems

If you have a problem with your electricity, gas or water supply, there's a 24-hour helpline. You can find the telephone number on the bill, in the phone book or in the Yellow Pages.

Gas & Electricity Suppliers

There is no one company supplying all the electricity or gas to UK households. Instead, you can choose between different electricity and gas suppliers. All have different terms and conditions, as well as different prices, and all are keen to get your business. This can be confusing, therefore you should do some research and obtain advice before signing a contract with a new supplier.

♦ To find out which company supplies your gas, call Transco on ☎ 0870-608 1524.

♦ To find out which company supplies your electricity and telephone service, call Energywatch (☎ 0845-906 0708), who can also advise you about changing your electricity or gas supplier.

Telephone

In the UK, most homes have a telephone, which is called a land line (as opposed to a mobile). If there's no line installed, you can get one from British Telecom (☎ 150442) or from a cable company. BT and other companies now offer many services, including land lines, mobile phone and internet services – you just choose what you need. The number of different services and prices can be confusing. Ofcom (🖥 www.ofcom.org.uk) provides advice about different tariffs (prices) and changing your telephone company.

To make calls outside the home, you can call from a public payphone using cash, a pre-paid phone card or use a credit or debit card (and, of course, use a mobile phone). The most expensive place to make a phone call is from a hotel or hostel.

To call the police, fire or ambulance service, dial ☎ 999 or 112. This is a free service but should **only** be used in a real emergency. There are non-emergency local numbers for these services in the phone book.

Bills

Bills are sent out by the suppliers of water, electricity, gas and telephone, and these provide

♢ All UK homes have water and electricity connected and most, but not all, have gas.

♢ The electricity supply in the UK is 240 volts.

♢ Who to contact to find out who supplies your gas and electricity – and for advice on telephone charges.

♢ The most expensive places to make phone calls from.

♢ How to contact the emergency services.

♢ What direct debits, standing orders and budget schemes are – and what the advantages are.

details about how to pay, usually on the back. If you have a bank account, the easiest way to pay bills is by direct debit or standing order – a direct or regular payment made to the company by your bank. This avoids problems if you forget to pay! Most utility companies offer budget schemes which allow you to pay a fixed amount each month.

Note that if you don't pay a bill, the service could be cut and you will have to pay a fee to get it reconnected.

Refuse Collection

Collecting refuse, also called rubbish or trash, is the responsibility of the local authority. Collections take place regularly, usually on the same day each week, and you must leave your refuse in a particular place to have it taken away. Different local authorities have different -*8/7s case, certain items, such as glass, paper, metals and plastic, must be separated from the rest of the refuse to be collected separately, sometimes on a different day. Recycling boxes are provided free of charge for these. Make sure you know what is collected and when – contact your local authority for information.

♦ Large objects, such as beds, wardrobes and fridges, need to be collected separately, and you must contact the local authority to arrange this (there may be a fee).

♦ Businesses, such as factories and shops, must make special arrangements with the local authority to have their refuse collected.

♦ You cannot just dump rubbish anywhere – known as 'fly-tipping' – as this is illegal.

Council Tax

Local government services, such as education, roads, refuse collection, libraries and the police service, are paid for partly by government grants and partly by the Council Tax (see **Local Government** on page 78). This tax is paid by every person (unless exempt) in England, Scotland and Wales (Northern Ireland has a different system, called domestic rates).

When you move into a property as the owner or as a tenant, you must register to pay Council Tax. The level of tax you pay depends on where the property is situated, its size and, most importantly, its value. The tax can be paid in one payment, in two biannual instalments or in ten monthly instalments from April to January.

Council Tax is often expensive, making it one of the most unpopular taxes in the UK, although there are reductions in certain circumstances:

♦ if only one person lives in the property, the tax is reduced by 25 per cent (this doesn't apply in Northern Ireland);

♦ if someone living in the property has a disability, reductions are also available.

People on a low income or those receiving benefits, such as Income

must know

♦ How refuse is collected and by whom.

♦ What is meant by recycling and which items may need to be recycled.

♦ What Council Tax pays for.

♦ How Council Tax is calculated – and how to pay it.

♦ What reductions are available and who qualifies.

Support or Jobseeker's Allowance, may receive Council Tax Benefit. Ask your local authority about this or contact a Citizens' Advice Bureau.

Buildings & Household Insurance

Insurance safeguards your house or flat and the possessions inside it against loss or damage, e.g. from flood, fire or theft. Most people in the UK insure their belongings. If you buy a home with a mortgage, the mortgage lender will insist you insure the building against fire, theft and accidental damage. Landlords arrange this insurance for rented buildings. Wherever you live, it's advisable to insure your possessions against theft or damage with one of the many companies providing insurance.

Neighbours

Your neighbours are the people who live next door and nearby, and most UK neighbours get along well, but occasionally there are problems. If you have a dispute with your neighbours, the first thing to do is to try discussing it with them. If this doesn't solve the problem and you live in rented accommodation, talk to whoever is providing your accommodation – the landlord, housing association or local authority. Always keep a record of problems in case you need to prove what happened and when it started. If neighbours cause a serious nuisance (create problems for you), they can be evicted (removed) from their home.

Some disputes (disagreements) between neighbours end up in court, but there are organisations which will mediate to try to prevent this by talking to both sides and trying to find a solution that's acceptable to both parties. Details of mediation organisations are available from your local authority, the Citizens' Advice Bureau and Mediation UK (☎ 0117-904 6661 or visit 🖳 www. mediationuk.co.uk).

must know

- What you may need insurance for.
- What to do if you have problems with your neighbours.

MONEY & CREDIT

The UK's currency is sterling – pounds (£) and pence (p) – with four banknotes and eight coins. The denominations (values) of the coins are: 1p, 2p, 5p, 10p, 20p, 50p, £1 and £2, with notes of £5, £10, £20 and £50.

Scotland and Northern Ireland have their own banknotes, which have the same values. Although they are legal tender (valid) throughout the UK, some shopkeepers don't know this and won't accept them. It's also difficult to exchange them abroad and it's best to avoid taking them out of the UK.

The Euro

The Euro has been the common (shared) currency of the European Union (EU) since January 2002 when 12 member states adopted it. The UK was not one of those states, and the UK government has said it will only adopt the Euro if the British vote to do so in a referendum – currently most British people prefer to keep the pound. There are Euros in circulation in the

UK, especially in Northern Ireland, close to the border with the Republic of Ireland where the Euro is the national currency.

Foreign Currency

Money can be changed and foreign currency can be purchased at banks, building societies, post offices and currency exchange shops (*bureaux de change*). Some currencies must be ordered in advance but many – including US dollars and Euros – are readily available. Exchange rates vary, so shop around for the best deal.

Banks & Building Societies

Most UK adults have an account with a bank or building society. It's difficult to manage without one, as most employers pay their employees' salaries directly into their bank accounts. There are plenty to choose from, and many large national banks and building societies have branches in towns throughout the UK. There's a lot of competition between banks and building societies, and even supermarkets and chain stores now offer banking services, plus a range of internet banks. They all offer a variety of different accounts, therefore you need to compare their fees and savings' interest rates to see what best suits you.

To open an account you must show:

♦ documents that prove your identity, such as a passport, immigration document or photo driving licence;

♦ documents that prove your address, such as a tenancy agreement or household utility bill.

Cash & Debit Cards

These are the cards issued by banks and building societies which allow you to withdraw (take out) your money. You can use them at the counter in the bank, in an automated teller machine (or ATM, often called a 'cashpoint' or 'hole in the wall'), or to pay for goods in shops without using cash. To use your card, you need a Personal Identification Number (PIN) which must be kept secret. The amount you spend is debited (taken) from your account, therefore you  must have enough money in your account to cover what you spend. If you lose your cash card or debit card, you must inform the bank immediately.

Credit & Store Cards

These cards can also be used to pay for things, in shops, on the telephone or over the internet – a store card is similar to a credit card, but you can only use it in branches of the store which issued it. Credit and store cards don't withdraw money directly from your bank account;

instead you're 'borrowing' the money from the company and will be sent a bill each month. If you lose your credit or store card, you must inform the company immediately.

Note that if you don't pay off the total amount each month, you will be charged interest. Credit and store cards are useful, but they can also be dangerous as they may tempt you to buy things and pay for them later. The interest rate is usually **very** high, and it's easy to get into debt if you don't pay off the full amount each month.

Credit & Loans

Sooner or later you may want to borrow money for a large purchase such as a car, household goods or a holiday. This type of borrowing is more common in the UK than in many other countries, and people often borrow from banks or other organisations – it's known as taking out a loan or obtaining credit. Check the terms and conditions carefully if you decide to take out a loan, and make sure that you can afford the repayments.

For advice about loans, contact a Citizens' Advice Centre.

Being Refused Credit

Not everyone who requests a loan receives one, and your application may be refused. Banks use a range of credit information to decide whether to lend you money, which includes your occupation and salary, your address and your previous credit record (how much you've borrowed and whether you paid the money back on time). If you're refused a loan you have the right to ask the reason why.

Credit Unions

Banks and building societies are not the only lenders. Credit unions are financial co-operatives that are owned and controlled by their members who pool (put together) their savings and then make loans to each other from this central fund. There are credit unions in most cities and towns, and interest on credit union loans is usually much lower than that charged by banks and building societies.

To find your nearest credit union, contact the Association of British Credit Unions (💻 www.abcul.coop).

Insurance

People in the UK insure their homes and possessions against loss or damage (see **Buildings & Household Insurance** on page 109), but insurance is also available for the following:

must know

- The different coins and notes which make up the UK's currency.

- When the EU started to use the Euro – and what must happen before Britain adopts it.

- Where to buy foreign currency.

- Why you need a bank or building society account – and what documents you need to open one.

- The differences between cash and debit cards and credit and store cards.

- Why credit and store cards can be dangerous.

- Why you might need a PIN number.

- What to do if you lose your cards.

♦ Cars and motorcycles – third party insurance is compulsory (essential) for a motor vehicle on the public road.

♦ Holidays – travel insurance compensates you for losing your luggage or pays for medical treatment abroad.

♦ Cameras, mobile phones and other personal items that are popular targets for thieves.

Insurance can be arranged directly with an insurance company or through an insurance broker, who will try to obtain the best deal.

Social Security

In the UK, money is available to help those who don't have enough money to live on. These are called welfare benefits, and are funded by the social security system. Benefits are available to several different groups of people, including those who are:

♦ sick or disabled

♦ elderly (older people)

♦ unemployed (people without a job)

♦ on a low income

must know

- That taking out a loan is common in the UK.

- Why you might be refused a loan.

- What a credit union is.

- The different types of insurance, and which are compulsory.

- What benefits are, who can claim them and who cannot.

- How to get help with benefits and debt.

You aren't able to claim benefits if you don't have the legal right of residence (or 'settlement') in the UK. The benefits system is complicated, as it covers a great many people in different situations. Advice on benefits is available from post offices and libraries, Jobcentre Plus offices and the Citizens' Advice Bureau.

HEALTH

People in the UK are proud of their National Health Service (NHS), which provides all residents with free healthcare and treatment. The NHS was established in 1948, and was the world's first national health service that provided free treatment to all citizens, and is now one of the largest organisations in Europe.

Doctors

Healthcare starts with the family doctor or general practitioner (GP), who's the first person you should see if you're ill. They may work alone in surgeries or with other GPs in large group practices, sometimes called Primary Health Care Centres (primary means first).

GPs organise their patients' treatment, which can be for physical or mental illnesses. If they cannot treat you themselves they will refer (direct) you to a specialist, usually in a hospital, and can also refer you for tests or treatment such as physiotherapy. You cannot just turn up at a hospital and expect to see a doctor or specialist without a referral from your GP – usually a GP's letter – unless it's an emergency. The only hospital department you can go to without a GP's referral is the Accident and Emergency (A&E) department. To find a GP in your area, you can ask your friends and neighbours to recommend a doctor. Alternatively, lists of local GPs are available at libraries, post offices, tourist information offices, local health authorities and Citizens' Advice Bureaux. The following websites are also useful.

- ◆ England – 🖳 www.nhs.uk

- ◆ Scotland – 🖳 www.show.scot.nhs.uk/findnearest/ healthservices

- ◆ Wales – 🖳 www.wales.nhs.uk/directory.cfm

- ◆ Northern Ireland – 🖳 www.n-i.nhs.uk

Registering with a GP

Don't wait until you're ill to find a doctor, but register (put your name down) with a GP as soon as you move to a new area. With luck, you should have a choice of doctors, so check which surgeries offer what you want: a female GP, for example, or maternity services. Some busy surgeries cannot accept new patients, but there will be others who can take you on. If you have problems finding a GP, ask your local health authority to find you one, which they must do by law.

Once you find a GP or group practice, the staff there will tell you how to register, which usually involves completing a form and producing your medical card. If you don't have a medical card, ask the receptionist for a form to send to the local health authority, who will issue you with a card.

All patients registering with a GP are entitled to a free health check, therefore you should make sure that you have one.

Using Your Doctor

You make an appointment to see your GP in person or by phone. GPs are busy people and you cannot always see your GP when you want to, and it may be necessary to wait several days or even see another GP at the same practice. If you're very ill and need to be seen immediately, you can ask for an urgent appointment.

You should try to make sure that you're at the surgery a few minutes before your appointment. If you cannot attend or don't need to see the doctor any more, you must let the surgery know so that another patient can take your place.

During your appointment, answer all the GP's questions as fully as you can, as he needs as much information as possible on order to assess what's wrong with you. Everything you tell him is confidential, which means that he cannot pass it on to anyone else, including your partner or family, without your permission. If you don't understand something, ask him to explain it.

If you can speak only limited English, you can take someone with you, or ask the GP's receptionist to arrange for an interpreter, when you make the appointment. Interpreters are expensive and the GP pays their fee, therefore if you cannot make the appointment, you must let the surgery know.

Home & Out-of-Hours Visits

If you're too ill to visit a GP's surgery you can ask for a home visit. Doctors visit patients at home in extreme circumstances and give priority to people who are unable to travel, e.g. the elderly or those confined to bed, so don't ask for a home visit if you don't really need one. If you need to see a GP out of hours, e.g. at night or over the weekend, you'll be asked a number of questions to assess how serious your case is. A doctor may come to your home or you may be advised to go to the nearest A&E department.

Charges & Prescriptions

Treatment at your GP's surgery and at a hospital is free, but you do have to pay for certain services, such as vaccinations (injections which protect you) for travel abroad. If the GP decides that you need medicine, he will write a prescription which you take to a pharmacy (chemist).

Although chemists sell a lot of 'over the counter' medicines (those for sale without a doctor's permission), others require a prescription. This is a written instruction from a doctor, including the medicine or drug, the dose (how much should be taken and when) and how it should be taken. The pharmacist dispenses (prepares) the medicine.

There's a charge for each prescribed medicine, but some people receive them free of charge, including the following:

♦ those aged under 16 (under 25 in Wales);

♦ anyone aged under 19 and in full-time education, such as college or university;

♦ those who are 60 or over;

♦ pregnant women, and mothers of babies under 12 months old;

♦ those suffering from a specified medical condition;

♦ anyone receiving certain welfare benefits such as Income Support, Jobseekers' Allowance, Working Families and Disabilities Tax Credit.

NHS Direct & Walk-in Centres

NHS Direct is a 24-hour telephone service (☎ 0845-4647 or ☎ 0845-424 2424 in Scotland) which you can call for information about health problems. You can also ask for an interpreter and receive advice in your own language.

NHS Direct Online is a website (🖳 www.nhsdirect.nhs.uk or 🖳 www.nhs24.com in Scotland), which provides information about health services and medical conditions.

NHS walk-in centres are places where you can receive treatment for minor injuries and illness without an appointment. To find your nearest walk-in centre, call NHS Direct (see above) or see the NHS website (💻 www.nhs.uk – click on 'local NHS services' – or visit 💻 www.n-i.nhs.uk in Northern Ireland).

Feeling Unwell: What You Should Do

If you or one of your family is ill, you have a number of options, which depend on the type of illness and how serious it is.

If you just need information or advice you can:

♦ talk to a pharmacist (chemist), who can give advice on less serious conditions and suggest over-the-counter medicines to treat them;

♦ speak to a nurse by phoning NHS Direct (☎ 0845-4647);

♦ visit the NHS Direct Online website (💻 www.nhsdirect.nhs.uk).

♦ If you need to see a doctor or nurse:

♦ make an appointment at your GP's surgery;

♦ visit an NHS walk-in centre.

♦ if you need urgent medical treatment:

♦ contact your GP;

♦ go straight to the nearest hospital with an Accident & Emergency (A&E) department;

♦ call 999 for an ambulance – **calls are free but you should only use this service in a real emergency.**

Hospitals

Many people are nervous about going into hospital, but UK hospitals have an excellent reputation for treatment and patient care. A patient is someone who receives treatment and, unlike the custom in some other countries, UK patients are looked after by nurses and other staff, rather than by your family. Because of this, visiting times may be limited.

You can be admitted to a hospital in one of three ways:

♦ **As an outpatient** – this means visiting the Outpatients department and seeing a specialist for a consultation or for minor tests.

♦ **As a day patient** – this means having treatment at a hospital which may last several hours. Day patients are discharged (released) and return home the same day.

must know

↻ What the National Health Service provides, and when it was founded.

↻ That the UK has a free healthcare system.

↻ How to find and register with a GP.

↻ How to see your GP and what he can do for you.

↻ What to do if you're too ill to visit your GP, or you need an out-of-hours visit.

↻ What prescriptions are, and who gets them free of charge.

↻ What NHS Direct, NHS Direct Online and NHS walk-in centres are.

♦ **As an in-patient** – this means you stay in a hospital bed at least for one night. In-patients need to take some personal belongings with them to hospital, such as night clothes, a dressing gown, towels and toiletries. You will receive all your meals from the hospital.

To learn more about going into hospital, contact Customer Services or the Patient Advice and Liaison Service (PALS) at the hospital where you will be receiving treatment.

Dentists

Dentists look after your teeth. Some work for the NHS while others have private practices, and many do both. Most people must pay for treatment, even with an NHS dentist (which is cheaper); most dentists have two sets of fees, a lower one for NHS patients and a higher one for private patients. It's advisable to try to get onto a dentist's NHS list as soon as possible, although there's a high demand for NHS dentists and this can be difficult or impossible in some areas. All dentists should explain the treatment – and how much it will cost – before treating you.
   You can get free dental treatment on the NHS if you're:

♦ aged under 18;

♦ living in Wales and aged under 25 or over 60;

♦ pregnant and/or have a baby aged under 12 months;

♦ receiving certain benefits, such as Income Support, Jobseekers' Allowance or Pension Credit Guarantee.

To find a dentist, ask your friends and neighbours for a recommendation, obtain a list of local dentists from the local library or Citizens' Advice Bureau, or contact NHS Direct.

Opticians

Opticians look after the health of your eyes, check your vision and prescribe spectacles and contact lenses. As with dentists, most people must pay for sight tests and glasses. Those who are treated free of charge include children, those aged over 60, people with certain eye conditions or conditions which may affect their eyesight, and those on certain benefits. NHS Direct can advise on this. In Scotland, all eye tests are free.

must know

⟁ The difference between an outpatient, a day patient and an in-patient.

⟁ Where to get advice about going into hospital.

⟁ The difference between an NHS and a private dentist – and where to find one.

⟁ What an optician does.

⟁ Who is eligible for free dental treatment and eye tests.

Pregnancy & the Care of Young Children

The NHS provides many services for mothers and babies, both before and after a birth.

Before the Birth

As soon as a woman discovers that she's pregnant she should tell her GP, who can also perform a pregnancy test to confirm the pregnancy and calculate the 'due date' (when the baby will arrive) and organise a range of ante-natal (before birth) services. These are available at local hospitals, health centres and special ante-natal clinics. There are also classes where women can learn exercises to help them during the birth.

Mothers-to-be also receive support from their GP and a midwife – a nurse who specialises in helping women through their pregnancy and birth. Not all GPs offer maternity services, therefore women may need to sign on with a different GP when pregnant.

Giving Birth

In the UK, the majority of women give birth in hospital, especially when it's their first baby. It's normal for the father to be there during the birth, but only if the mother wants him there.

After the Birth

Soon after a child is born, the family will be contacted by a health visitor: a specially qualified nurse who checks that both mother and baby are doing well and advises about caring for a new baby. He or she will visit you at home to begin with, but later you may meet your health visitor at a clinic. You stay in contact with the health visitor until the child is five years old and ready to start school.

Additional support is available at mother and toddler (small children aged up to three) groups or playgroups for young children, which are often held at local churches and community centres – these are a good place to meet other parents. As your child gets older, you can send him or her to a nursery school.

Information About Pregnancy

There are several different places and organisations where you can obtain information about pregnancy, birth and looking after a new baby:

♦ Maternity and ante-natal services in your area – contact your GP, a health visitor or your local health authority. The number is in the phone book.

♦ Contraception (ways to prevent unwanted pregnancy) and sexual health – for advice contact the Family Planning Association (☎ 0845-310 1334, 🖥 www.fpa.org.uk.

♦ Pregnancy, childbirth and early parenthood – for advice and support, see the National Childbirth Trust website (🖥 www.nctpregnancyandbabycare.com).

Registering a Birth

The UK has an official Register (list) of Births, Marriages and Deaths, so it can keep track of the population. All babies must be registered within six weeks of their birth, which is done at the Register Office (the address is in the phone book). You will receive a birth certificate for the baby and must keep this safe.

Your personal circumstances will indicate who should register the birth, as follows:

- If the parents are married, either can register the birth.

- If the parents aren't married only the mother can register the birth.

- If the parents are unmarried but want both their names on the birth certificate, both must attend to register the birth.

must know

- Where to find help, advice and treatment when you're pregnant and after the baby is born.

- Where most British women give birth.

- What a midwife does.

- What a health visitor does and how long you're in contact with them.

- How, when and where you register a baby's birth.

EDUCATION

Education is free in the UK for children aged five to 18. It's also compulsory for all children between the ages of five and 16 (four and 16 in Northern Ireland): this means that children **must** attend school between those ages. The education system varies in England, Scotland, Wales and Northern Ireland – the main regional differences are highlighted in this section.

Schools

Children start school when they're five (four in Northern Ireland). Their parent or guardian (a person who has legal responsibility for the child) must make sure that their child goes to school, arrives on time and attends classes for the whole school year. If a child isn't in school when he should be, the parent/guardian can be prosecuted (taken to court). This includes any days during the school term that children are absent (away) from school without a good reason, e.g. illness. The school system is divided into a number of different stages or levels:

Nursery school – this is optional (children don't have to attend) and in some parts of the country it's free for children over three.

Primary school – children attend at different ages depending on where they live.

- In England and Wales this stage lasts from five to 11.

- In Scotland from five to 12.

- In Northern Ireland from four to 11.

Middle school – this is an option between primary and secondary school, and is available in some parts of the UK. Children attend between the ages of eight and 13, and then go to secondary (senior) school until they're 16.

Secondary school – children continue their education until they're 17. At that age they can leave school or continue until they're 18.

You can obtain details of all local schools from your local education authority (LEA) office or website – see your phone book for contact details.

Primary Schools

Primary schools are usually mixed (boys and girls together) and close to a child's home. Children are usually grouped by age into classes and have all their lessons within that group, often with the same teacher. Parents are encouraged to help their children to learn at home, especially with basic skills such as reading and writing.

Secondary Schools

This stage of a child's education begins at 11 (12 in Scotland). Secondary schools are larger than primary schools and while most are mixed sex, a few are single-sex schools (girls or boys).

Children may go to the secondary school nearest their home, but could also travel to one further away – it depends on their parents' preferences and the number of school places available. Some secondary schools have a better reputation for attendance and examination results than others, and are more popular with parents. However, it can be difficult to get a place in a popular school, therefore parents may apply to several different schools. If their first choice of school has enough places, their child will be admitted (offered a place); if not, children are offered places according to the school's admission arrangements, which vary, depending on the local education authority.

It isn't unusual for parents to choose to live in or move to the catchment area (area from where children can be admitted) of a particularly good school, as children living there are more likely to be offered a place. The system in Northern Ireland is different, and many schools there select pupils through a test, which children take at the age of 11.

If you have a child who is close to secondary school age, ask your local education authority for information about schools in your area, which schools have places and how to apply. It will also advise on the admission arrangements; for example, why

must know

- ☞ The ages when education is compulsory, and the role of parents and guardians.

- ☞ The ages between which state education is free.

- ☞ The different types of schools and the ages of children who attend them.

- ☞ The difference between mixed sex and single-sex schools.

- ☞ How to obtain a place in a secondary school.

- ☞ The items and activities which parents have to pay for – and how to get help with this.

some children will be given a place when there are only a few available, and why other children might not.

Costs

Education is free in UK state schools, but parents must pay for certain items, such as the school uniform and sports wear. They may also have to contribute towards activities, such as school outings and music lessons. If parents don't earn much money, financial help is available, and a child may also receive free school meals. (School meals aren't usually compulsory, and many children take a packed lunch instead.) The local education authority or Citizens' Advice Bureau can advise on this.

Church & Other Faith Schools

Some schools in the UK are linked to certain religions and are known as church schools or 'faith schools'. Most of these are Church of England or Roman Catholic church schools, although they don't expect children to come from particularly religious families. There are also Muslim, Jewish and Sikh schools in some areas. Northern Ireland has some schools that aim to bring children of different religions together, called Integrated Schools. You can obtain more information about faith schools from your local education authority.

Independent Schools

Independent schools are private schools which aren't run or paid for by the state. Confusingly, these schools are also sometimes referred to as 'public schools'. There are around 2,500 independent schools in the UK attended by around eight per cent of Britain's children. Parents pay the entire cost of their child's education, although some schools offer scholarships to gifted (talented) children, which cover some or all of the cost of his or her education.

The Curriculum

Britain's National School Curriculum sets out the subjects that must be taught in all state primary and secondary schools in England, Wales and Northern Ireland, ensuring that all children receive the same standard of education. These subjects are:

English	Geography
Maths	Modern foreign languages
Science	Art and design
Design and technology	Music
Information and communication technology (ICT)	Physical education (PE)
History	Citizenship

There are regional variations. For example, in Wales children learn Welsh and in some primary schools all lessons are taught in Welsh, while Scotland has its own broad national curriculum.

- What faith schools and Integrated Schools are.

- How many independent schools there are in the UK and what percentage of children attend them.

- Which subjects are included in the National Curriculum.

- Which subject must all schools teach, by law, but which children don't have to attend.

The law says that all schools must also teach religious education (RE) to all pupils, although parents can withdraw their children from RE lessons. RE is based upon Christianity, but other major religions are also covered.

Assessment

Assessments are tests and examinations which take place throughout a child's education to check how much they've learned and to highlight and deal with any areas of weakness. The different regions take a different approach to assessment.

England: the curriculum is divided into four Key Stages, with tests after each stage. These tests, which are also called SATs (Scholastic Assessment Test), take place when a child is 7, 11 and 14. And then at age 16, they usually take the General Certificate of Education (GCSE) in a number of subjects. A few schools offer alternative qualifications. Young people may stay on at school to take further qualifications, called Advanced GCE levels (AGCEs or A levels). The results of these may decide if and where they go on to study in higher education.

Wales: schools follow the Welsh National Curriculum, but children no longer have to take SATs tests at ages 7 and 11, although teachers must still assess and report on pupils' progress at those ages. There are also plans to stop testing 14-year-olds.

Scotland: the education system is quite different from that of England and Wales, with even less emphasis on examinations. Currently, the curriculum is divided into two phases:

◆ The first phase covers children aged from five to 14, and consists of six levels – Levels A to F. There are no large group tests during this time; instead teachers test individual children when they think they're ready, therefore children develop at their own speed.

◆ The second phase is more intensive, as children aged 14 to 16 study for Standard Grade. After 16, they can go on to study at intermediate, higher or advanced level.

Scotland is planning to change to a single curriculum, which will apply to all children from the age of three right up to young adults of 18. It's been called 'A Curriculum for Excellence' (www.acurriculumforexcellencescotland.gov.uk).

Help with English

Not all children speak English as their first language. If your child's mother tongue isn't English, extra help is available from a specialist teacher, called an English Additional Language (EAL) teacher.

Careers Education

'What do you want to be when you grow up?' Children in England start getting help to answer that question from a young age. Careers advice is available in Scotland to children of any age. In Wales, it begins once they're 11 and in England at age 14. There's usually a wealth of information available about all sorts of career options, with specialist staff to help.

There are also organisations offering young people careers guidance:

◆ Connexions, a nationwide service in England (☎ 080-800 13219 or 🖳 www.connexions-direct.com);

◆ Careers Wales (☎ 0800-100900 or 🖳 www.careerswales.com);

◆ Careers Scotland (☎ 0845-850 2502 or 🖳 www.careers-scotland.org.uk).

Parents & Schools

Most UK parents are keen to be involved in their children's education, and schools engage them in several different ways:

◆ Joining the school's governing body – there are places kept for parents in this organisation which decides how a school is run and administered, and produces annual reports on the progress of the school. In Scotland, there are places for parents on similar bodies, such as school boards and parent councils.

◆ Enlisting parents' support – schools ask parents to sign a 'home-school agreement' which is a list of things both the school and the parents agree to in order for their child to have the best possible education. These include ensuring a child attends the full school year – schools must be open 190 days a year, although the term times are decided locally by the governing body and education authority – as well as informing the school when a child will be absent from school.

◆ Keeping parents informed – each year parents receive a report on a child's progress and an invitation to visit the school and talk to the teachers.

Further Education & Adult Education

Education in Britain isn't just for children, and there's plenty of opportunities to continue learning for the rest of your life.

must know

- What assessment consists of, and how it differs across the regions.

- When children take SATs tests in England, Wales and Northern Ireland.

- How the Scottish education system differs, and how it is changing.

- What help is available to children who don't speak English as their first language.

- When careers education starts – and the organisations which provide it.

- The different ways parents can be involved in their child's school and education.

- What a school's governing body does.

- What a 'home-school agreement' is.

After School – after the age of 17, young people are free to leave school. Some will go out to work, while others choose to stay in full-time education. Many take A levels (Higher Grades in Scotland) to prepare for university, while others go to a college of further education (FE) to improve their examination grades or to work towards career qualifications.

Most FE courses are free up to the age of 19; and the government encourages young people from low-income families to continue their education by providing financial help to those who carry on their studies after leaving school at 16, called an Education Maintenance Allowance (EMA). Find out more at your local college or contact 🖳 www.dfes.gov.uk.

Adult Education – there are many courses available to over 18s. Some concentrate on improving basic skills such as literacy (reading and writing) and numeracy (working with numbers), or on gaining new skills for employment. Others are for people who need to improve their English language skills, called ESOL (English for Speakers of Other Languages). ESOL courses are also available at community centres and training centres. They are popular, as there's increasing pressure on immigrants to improve their knowledge of English, therefore there's sometimes a waiting list to get onto a course. In England and Wales, ESOL, literacy and numeracy courses are also called 'Skills for Life' courses. Find out more at your local college or library, or phone Learndirect (☎ 0800-100900).

Some ESOL courses are combined with citizenship, and a pass certificate is the equivalent of passing the 'Life in the UK' test. If you're struggling with this book, you may need to consider taking an ESOL course. Courses must be recognised by Directgov and/or Learndirect, and these organisations are the best place to start looking. Any course offering to get you to the required standard of English in a week or less is unlikely to provide the desired certificate; and without it, you risk being turned down for citizenship or ILR (settlement).

Skills & Hobbies – not all courses are about qualifications. Some offer the chance to learn a new skill or hobby, and to meet new people. You can take up a new sport, learn a new language or even how to play a musical instrument. These courses are often called evening classes, as many take place after work. Find out more from your local library, college or adult education centre.

University

University is more popular in the UK than ever before, and not just with young people. Although young people often go to university after taking their A levels (or Higher grades in Scotland), many adults choose to study in later life, either on a full-time or a part-time basis.

Paying for University

Unfortunately, a university education isn't free – or even cheap. Many students have to borrow money to pay for tuition fees and living expenses.

Fees: universities can charge up to £3,000 a year for tuition. The government pays this to begin with (via grants and student loans), so students don't have to meet this cost before or during university. However, they have to repay their student loan as soon as they start working (depending on their income). In Scotland, there are no tuition fees; however, students still pay back some of the cost of their education with a payment called an endowment.

Living Expenses: the cost of accommodation, food, books and the odd night out all add up, and many students take out a bank loan to cover these costs – like the government's student loan, this is repaid once they're working. Others take a part-time job while they're studying to help with their living expenses.

Financial Help: grants are available to help low-income families with their children's university tuition fees. Universities also help with bursaries, which are awards made to students to help them with study costs, such as travel, equipment and books.

must know

- The kind of courses available at a further education (FE) college.
- The financial help available to over 16s from low-income families who continue their education.
- Where you can take English classes or other skills-based courses.
- What ESOL means.
- Who goes to university and who pays for it.
- The cost of university tuition – and how you can get help.

LEISURE

There's no shortage of things to do in the UK in the evenings and at weekends, and whenever you have spare time. Sports, the arts and other entertainment give countless opportunities, including the following:

- ◆ museums and art galleries – many of these are free;
- ◆ cinema, theatre and concerts – all the major movies and entertainers come to the UK;
- ◆ exhibitions on subjects as diverse as sailing, fashion and food;
- ◆ walking – the UK has an extensive network of footpaths;
- ◆ visiting heritage sites – many of these are maintained by the National Trust (💻 www. nationaltrust.org.uk).

Information

Local newspapers feature information and listings of what's on at theatres, cinemas, music and exhibition venues. Tourist information offices and libraries also have up-to-date news and there are also numerous entertainment websites.

Film, Video & DVD

The UK has a system of film classification to indicate which films are suitable for children, and which should only be viewed by adults. If a child is below the age shown on the classification, they shouldn't watch a film at a cinema – they probably won't be allowed in anyway – or at home on video or DVD.

Films are classified as follows:

♦ **U** (Universal) – suitable for anyone aged four or over.

♦ **PG** (parental guidance) – suitable for everyone, but there parts of the film which might be unsuitable for young children. It's up to their parents to decide.

♦ **12** or **12a** – children under 12 may only watch or rent these films if they're with an adult.

♦ **15** – children under 15 cannot watch or rent these films.

♦ **18** – only available to those aged 18 or over.

♦ **R18** – restricted 18 films can only be viewed by adults 18 or over in a cinema with a special licence.

Television & Radio

There's a huge amount of news, information and entertainment on British television (TV) and radio, with five main channels and dozens more if you have a satellite or cable connection.

If you want to watch TV, you must have a television licence. It's illegal to have a TV, DVD, video recorder, computer or any device which can be used for watching or recording TV programmes without a valid licence. If you don't have a TV licence you risk being prosecuted – there are special vans which detect television signals at homes where records show there's no licence! One licence covers all the TVs at a single address, therefore you can have a TV in each room if you wish. An exception is a shared house, where individuals renting separate rooms must each have their own licence.

A colour TV licence costs £139.50 for 12 months (in 2008), but you can pay in instalments. Blind people are given a 50 per cent discount and those aged 75 or over can apply for a free licence. You can buy your licence from a Pay Point outlet (shops and post offices where certain bills can be paid) or from TV Licensing, Bristol, BS98 1TL (☎ 0870-576 3763, 🖳 www.tvlicensing.co.uk).

Pubs & Nightclubs

The British are known for their love of pubs – or public houses. These are bars where people from the local community come together to socialise. They usually open from late morning or midday until 11pm; to stay open later, they must obtain a

♂ Some of the leisure options in the UK and where to find out about them.

♂ The different film classifications – and which films are suitable for children to watch.

♂ What a television licence is and who needs to buy one.

special licence. Nightclubs open and close later than pubs

Both pubs and clubs serve alcohol, but only those aged 18 or over may drink on the premises. The landlord (who runs the pub) can allow youngsters aged 14 or over to come into a pub, but they aren't allowed to drink alcohol. Once they're 16, they may drink wine or beer – but not spirits, such as whisky or gin – with a meal in a hotel or restaurant. However, they still aren't permitted to buy alcohol of any sort in a supermarket or off-licence (a shop selling alcohol) until they're 18.

must know

- What age you must be to drink alcohol in a pub or nightclub – or wine or beer with a restaurant meal.

- The minimum age for buying a lottery ticket or going into a gambling club.

- The laws which control pet-ownership and the treatment of animals.

Betting & Gambling

Like many countries, the UK has a National Lottery with huge weekly prizes (millions of pounds). There are also scratch cards offering the chance of an instant win. You must be 16 or over to buy a lottery ticket or scratch card. More serious gambling venues such as betting shops – where you can place bets on horse races and other events – and gambling clubs are closed to anyone under 18.

Pets

The British are a nation of animal lovers and many people have pets, which usually live in their homes. Dogs and cats are especially popular. The government encourages responsible pet ownership and there are laws which reinforce this. Dogs must be kept under control in public places, where they must also wear a collar showing the name and address of their owner. Owners are also responsible for cleaning up after their pets, and it's against the law to allow your dog to make a mess on the street or in a park and not clean up after it. With such affection for animals, it's no surprise that neglecting (failing to care for) a pet and treating it cruelly is a criminal offence.

Animal doctors are called veterinarians (or vets), who provide medical treatment and vaccinations. Vets' fees can be expensive – there's no NHS for your pets – although there's a charity for pet-owners who cannot afford to pay a vet, called the People's Dispensary for Sick Animals (www.pdsa.org.uk).

TRAVEL & TRANSPORT

Britain has an extensive public transport system, although it can be expensive and isn't always reliable. Most people who can afford it prefer to drive their own car.

Trains, Buses & Coaches

You must have a ticket to travel on public transport. Usually, you buy a ticket before getting on a train or an underground (subway or tube) system such as the London Underground. Bus tickets can be purchased as you board (get on) a bus, while coach tickets are generally bought in advance. Failure to buy or show a ticket when asked by a ticket inspector will result in a fine or even prosecution. The fare (the amount you pay) depends on the day and time – and the distance – you travel. Certain times of day, such as the rush hour (when people are going to or from work) may be more expensive, but discount (cheaper) tickets are available for the following people:

♦ families travelling together;

♦ people aged 60 or over;

♦ disabled people;

♦ students aged under 26.

There are many sources of information on timetables and fares for the different kinds of public transport across the UK.

Trains: call the National Rail Enquiry Service (☎ 0845-748 4950, 🖥 www.nationalrail.co.uk) or Translink in Northern Ireland (☎ 028-9066 6630, 🖥 www.translink.co.uk).

Buses – to obtain information about local bus schedules phone ☎ 0870-608250.

Coaches – the UK's largest coach network is National Express (☎ 0870-580 8080, 🖥 www. nationalexpress.com). For coaches in Scotland, contact Scottish Citylink (☎ 0870-550 5050, 🖥 www.citylink.co.uk.) and for Northern Ireland visit 🖥 www.translink.co.uk.

must know

↻ How to find out about trains, buses and coaches.

↻ Where to buy tickets.

↻ Why you shouldn't use an unlicensed minicab.

Taxis

London is famous for its black cabs, although there are taxis throughout the UK. There are taxi ranks outside railway stations and airports, and often in the centre of towns and cities, also. All taxis must, by law, be licensed and display a licence plate. This applies to black cabs and minicabs (cars which are used as taxis), and the licence plate should be clearly visible. Unlicensed taxis aren't insured to carry fare-paying passengers and aren't always safe. Women should never travel in unlicensed minicabs.

Driving

You need a licence to drive a motor vehicle on public roads and there are minimum ages for driving different vehicles, as follows:

♦ To drive a car or ride a motorcycle you must be aged 17 or over.

♦ To drive a medium-sized lorry you must be aged 18 or over.

To drive a large lorry or bus you must be aged 21 or over.

In addition, you need a special licence to drive a lorry, minibus or bus with more than eight passenger seats.

The Driving Licence

The only way to obtain a UK driving licence is to pass a driving test. There are plenty of driving schools and qualified instructors, but the test is quite complicated and can take a while to pass. There are three steps to obtaining a full driving licence:

1. Apply for a provisional licence, which is a licence that allows you to drive a motorcycle up to 125cc or a car. Learner drivers cannot drive on a motorway and must be accompanied at all times by someone aged over 21 who has held a full driving licence for at least three years. Other drivers need to know that you're a learner, therefore you must display special 'L' plates (or 'D' plates in Wales) on the vehicle. The form to apply for a provisional driving licence is available at post offices.

2. Take and pass a written theory test, which is a multiple choice test taken on a computer.

3. Take and pass a practical driving test, which is taken in a car on public roads with an examiner.

Once you pass your test and receive your full driving licence, it's valid until you're 70, when it must be renewed every three years. There's a special rule in Northern Ireland, where you must display an R-Plate (R stands for registered driver) for one year after passing the test.

Overseas Licences

You can use a foreign driving licence in the UK, but the amount of time you can drive with it may be limited. If the licence was issued in a European Union (EU) country, or in Iceland, Norway or Liechtenstein, you can drive in the UK for as long as the licence is valid and don't need to take a UK driving test. If the licence was issued outside the EU, you may use it for up to one year. This gives you time to obtain a UK provisional licence and pass both the written and practical driving tests. If you don't, you'll be unable to drive after 12 months has expired.

Insurance

Motor insurance is compulsory in the UK, where it's illegal to have a car without proper motor insurance or to let someone drive your car if they aren't insured to use it. There are large fines for drivers who break these laws.

Road Tax & MOT

All vehicle owners must pay a tax to drive their car or ride their motorbike on British roads. When you pay road tax, you receive a road tax disc which must be displayed in the windscreen and shows that the car is taxed. Without this, you risk having your car clamped or towed away. Road tax can be purchased at a post office.

Any vehicle over three years old must also pass a Ministry of Transport (MOT) test, which tests whether it's mechanically safe to drive. There are approved garages that carry out tests and, if your car passes, issue the MOT certificate. It's illegal to drive a car without an MOT certificate, as without one, your insurance isn't valid and your car will be uninsured.

must know

- The minimum ages for driving a motorcycle, car and other vehicles on UK roads.

- How to obtain a UK driving licence.

- What are the limits of driving on a provisional driving licence.

- What are the limits of driving on a foreign driving licence.

Safety

There are a number of safety rules which apply to all drivers and motorbike riders, including the following:

- Everyone in a vehicle, including children, must wear a seatbelt. Children under 12 may need a special booster cushion so that the seatbelt fits properly.

- All motorcyclists and their passengers must wear a crash helmet. The only exceptions to this law are Sikh men who wear a turban.

- It's illegal to use a mobile phone while driving.

Speed Limits

In such a crowded country as the UK, roads are busy and speed limits apply everywhere. There are also speed cameras everywhere! Ignore them and you may receive a penalty fine, as well as penalty points on your licence.

For cars and motorcycles, the speed limits are:

- **30 miles per hour** (mph) in built-up areas, unless a sign shows a different limit;

- **60 mph** on single carriageways (roads with one lane in each direction);

- **70 mph** on motorways and dual carriageways (roads with two or more lanes in each direction).

Speed limits are lower for buses, lorries (trucks) and cars towing (pulling) caravans.

Drink-driving

One of the most serious crimes you can commit on UK roads is drink-driving. It's illegal to drive if you're over the alcohol limit or drunk, and the penalties are severe. People who drink and drive are likely to be disqualified (banned) from driving for a long time. If police suspect you've been drinking, they can stop you and give you a test to check how much alcohol you have in your body, which involves blowing into a machine, called a breathalyser test.

If you're 'over the limit' – that is you have more than the permitted amount of alcohol in your blood – or you refuse to take a breathalyser test, the police will arrest you.

Accidents

If you're unlucky enough to be involved in a road accident, here's what you should do:

◆ Stop! Never drive away without stopping, as this is a criminal offence.

◆ If someone is injured you must call the police and ambulance – dial 999.

◆ Take the names, addresses, vehicle registration numbers (this identifies the car) and insurance details of the other drivers.

◆ Give your details to the other drivers – you may also have to give them to the police.

◆ Note down everything that happened and contact your insurance company as soon as possible.

◇ What insurance, road tax and the MOT are – and how to obtain them.

◇ Important safety rules and speed limits.

◇ What may happen if you drink and drive.

◇ What to do if you have an accident.

Even if the accident was your fault, it's better not to say this – if you admit fault then your insurance company may not pay. Let the insurance company decide whose fault it was!

IDENTITY DOCUMENTS

The UK has no identity (ID) card system as yet, however the government has plans to introduce ID cards in the next few years.

Proving Your Identity

Although you don't have to carry an ID card, you do have to prove your identity in certain situations, for example:

◆ opening a bank or building society account;

◆ renting accommodation;

◆ enrolling for a college course;

◆ hiring a car;

◆ applying for benefits, such as Housing Benefit;

◆ applying for a marriage certificate.

Documents which can be used as proof of identity (ID) include:

♦ a passport or travel document;

♦ official documents issued by the Home Office which show your immigration status;

♦ a certificate of identity;

♦ a provisional or full driving licence;

♦ a recent utility (electricity, gas or telephone) bill which shows your name and address;

♦ a rent or benefits book.

It may be necessary to use more than one of the above to prove your identity.

↻ That the UK has no official identity (ID) card – yet!

↻ Situations in which you might have to prove your identity – and the documents which can help you to do this.

WORDS TO LEARN

Check that you understand this chapter's key terms:

Housing

priority
accommodation, property
loan, mortgage
lender, repayment,
building society
estate agent
vendor
subject to contract, legally binding
solicitor
surveyor, survey
social housing, council housing
points basis
housing association, not-for-profit
organisation
shared ownership
landlord
letting agent
tenancy, tenancy agreement, lease
deposit, inventory
discriminate
homelessness, intentionally homeless
charity
Social Fund, Community Care Grant

Services in & for the home

utilities

water rates
instalment
meter, meter reading
land line
tariff, bill
direct debit, standing order, budget
scheme
refuse (rubbish)
recycling
fly-tipping
Council Tax
benefits
insurance
nuisance, evicted
dispute, mediation

Money & Credit

currency, sterling, denomination
valid
referendum
bureau de change, exchange rate
bank account, withdraw
debit card, cash card
PIN number
credit card
loan, credit
credit union

insurance broker
social security
welfare benefits

Health

National Health Service (NHS)
general practitioner (GP)
Primary Health Care Centre
specialist
refer, referral
Accident and Emergency (A&E)
Department
health authority
medical card
appointment
confidential
home visit, out-of-hours visit
vaccination
prescription, 'over the counter' medicine
pharmacy
outpatient, day patient, in-patient
optician
maternity, ante-natal
midwife, health visitor
Register Office

Education

guardian
absent
primary school, secondary school
local education authority
admission, catchment area
faith school, integrated school
independent school, 'public school'
scholarship

curriculum
assessment, examination
SATs, GCSEs, A levels
school governing body
'home-school agreement'
further education (FE)
Education Maintenance Allowance (EMA)
literacy, numeracy
ESOL, Skills for Life
tuition, endowment, bursary

Leisure

film classification
universal, parental guidance
television licence
pay point outlet
public house (pub), off-licence
national lottery, scratch card, betting shop
veterinarian

Travel & Transport

public transport
fare, timetable, rush hour
black cab, minicab
driving licence
provisional licence, L plates
theory test, practical test
road tax, MOT
penalty fine, penalty points
drink-driving
disqualified, 'over the limit', breathalyser
test

Identity Documents

identity card, ID card

PRACTICE QUESTIONS

Now test your knowledge of everyday needs with these practice questions. Make sure you can answer them all before you take your test.

1. **What proportion of the British population own their own homes?**

    A   Half
    B   Two thirds
    C   Three quarters
    D   One quarter

2. **For how many years do you have to repay most mortgages?**

    A   One year
    B   50 years
    C   10 years
    D   25 years

3. **Which of the following statements is correct?**

    A   Estate agents represent the person who is buying a property.
    B   Estate agents represent the person who is selling a property.

4. **In Scotland, a buyer who wishes to purchase a house or flat makes an offer which is lower than the asking price. True or false?**

5. **Why might you need the services of a surveyor?**

    A   **To check that a property is structurally sound**
    B   To check that a property has no legal problems
    C   To arrange your mortgage
    D   To find you a place to rent

6. **What is the housing provided by local authorities most often called?**

    A   Local housing
    B   Council housing
    C   Public housing
    D   Sheltered housing

7. **Which of the following statements is true?**

   A   Everyone is entitled to register for local authority housing but it can be difficult to obtain a home.
   B   Only people with special needs or on welfare benefits are entitled to register for local authority housing.

8. **What is an inventory?**

   A   A list of available rental properties
   B   A list of the contents in a rental property
   C   An agreement between a tenant and a landlord
   D   A list of rules that must be followed while living in a rental property

9. **Your landlord will give you your deposit back at the end of your tenancy, regardless of the condition of the property. True or false?**

10. **How long do most tenancies last?**

   A   Two years
   B   Three months
   C   One year
   D   Six months

11. **When can landlords legally discriminate against potential tenants?**

   A   When they or a relative of theirs will be sharing the accommodation
   B   When they feel like it
   C   When potential tenants have children under 16
   D   When they rent out more than one property

12. **Under which of the following circumstances may a council offer a homeless person somewhere to live? Give two answers.**

   A   They ask nicely
   B   They have family living in the area
   C   They have chronic ill health
   D   They left rented accommodation without paying the rent

13. **What must you remember to do when you move into a new property or out of an old one?**

   A   Turn off the gas and electricity
   B   Reset the gas and electricity meters
   C   Make a note of the electricity and gas meter readings
   D   Take the gas and electricity meters with you

14. **You can buy your gas and electricity from many different suppliers in the UK. True or false?**

15. **What is a land line?**

    A   A line connecting two houses
    B   A telephone line installed in a property
    C   An electricity connection
    D   A line in the road outside your home

16. **Who should you consult about the different services and prices offered by telephone companies?**

    A   The Citizens' Advice Bureau
    B   The council
    C   Ofcom
    D   Transco

17. **What is the emergency number for ambulances, the fire service and police? Give two answers.**

    A   911
    B   999
    C   112
    D   100

18. **What is the main advantage of paying your bills by direct debit?**

    A   It's cheaper than paying cash
    B   The payment is automatic so you don't forget to pay
    C   It's easier to budget for your bills
    D   The supplier offers you a better service

19. **What does the amount of Council Tax you pay depend upon?**

    A   The size of a property
    B   A property's value
    C   The location of a property
    D   All the above reasons

20. **Buildings and contents insurance is compulsory in the UK. True or false?**

21. **When will Britain adopt the Euro?**

   A   Never
   B   In 2010
   C   Only if the British people vote to adopt it in a referendum
   D   Only if the government decides to adopt it

22. **Which identity documents could you use to open a bank or building society account? Give two answers from the list below.**

   A   Passport
   B   Library card
   C   Birth certificate
   D   Utility bill

23. **What does PIN stand for?**

   A   Personal Investment Number
   B   Personal Identification Number
   C   Prime Identification Number
   D   Personal Identification Name

24. **If you pay for something by credit card, the money is taken straight out of your bank account. True or false?**

25. **Who cannot claim social security benefits?**

   A   People who work
   B   People who are unemployed
   C   People aged over 18 or under 60
   D   People with no legal right to UK residency

26. **What is the term GP short for?**

   A   General Practitioner
   B   General Patients
   C   Great Practitioner
   D   General Practice

27. **Which of the following statements is true?**

   A   If you're unwell you can go straight to a hospital and see a doctor.
   B   If you're unwell you must first see your GP and get a referral to hospital, if necessary.

28.   **How much does it cost to see a GP?**

    A   £50 an hour
    B   £5 per appointment
    C   Nothing
    D   It depends on how ill you are

29.   **If an individual or someone in their care feels unwell, should they dial 999 straight away?**

    A   Yes
    B   Only if it's a real emergency
    C   Only if they can't through to NHS Direct
    D   Yes, if it's between 9pm and 6am

30.   **Who doesn't have to pay for a prescription? Give two answers.**

    A   Anyone who is registered with a GP
    B   Anyone who is aged over 60
    C   Anyone claiming certain benefits, such as Income Support
    D   Anyone who's friends with the pharmacist

31.   **Someone who attends a hospital for minor tests is called an outpatient. True or false?**

32.   **Which of the following statements is true?**

    A   Dentists charge the same rate for treating NHS and private patients.
    B   Dentists don't charge the same rate for NHS patients as they do for private patients.

33.   **Where do UK women usually have babies?**

    A   At home
    B   In a birthing pool
    C   In hospital
    D   In a maternity clinic

34.   **A health visitor is available to advise parents on childcare until a child is what age?**

    A   10
    B   5
    C   2
    D   12 months

35. **The Family Planning Association provides advice on which subjects? Give two answers.**

    A   Sexual health
    B   Giving birth
    C   Preventing unwanted pregnancy
    D   Preventing family arguments

36. **How soon after the birth must a new baby be registered?**

    A   Within 12 weeks
    B   Within six months
    C   Within 12 months
    D   Within six weeks

37. **School attendance is compulsory for children in England, Scotland and Wales between which ages?**

    A   4 and 12
    B   5 and 17
    C   3 and 15
    D   4 and 18

38. **How many stages is compulsory education divided into in the UK?**

    A   Two or three
    B   Two
    C   Three
    D   Four

39. **What is a 'public school'?**

    A   A school to which all members of the public can send their children.
    B   A school which is paid for by public funds
    C   An independent school which charges parents fees
    D   An independent school which is free to children living in the school's catchment area

40. **There are special schools for the children brought up in certain religions, such as Roman Catholics, Jews and Muslims. True or false?**

41. **What is the short name for Key Stage tests?**

    A   A levels
    B   SATs
    C   GCSEs
    D   SITs

42. **Which of the following subjects is not a part of the UK's National School Curriculum?**

    A   Geography
    B   Food technology
    C   English
    D   Citizenship

43. **Which of the following statements is true?**

    A   In Scotland, children are assessed when teachers think they're ready and then tested when they're 16.
    B   In Scotland, children are tested when they are aged 7, 11 and 14.

44. **At what age can children either leave school or stay on and study for further examinations?**

    A   14
    B   15
    C   16
    D   17

45. **Parents can be prosecuted if their child fails to attend school. True or false?**

46. **What does ESOL stand for?**

    A   English School of Language
    B   Everyday Skills of Learning
    C   English for Speakers of Other Languages
    D   Exam Skills or Lessons

47. **What is the average cost of a year's tuition at a UK university?**

    A   £3,000
    B   £300
    C   Nothing – the government pays
    D   It's up to the student to make a donation

48. **Films with a 'PG' rating are suitable for who?**

    A   Parents and guardians only
    B   Everyone – it means the film is 'particularly good'
    C   Everyone, but parents should decide whether or not it's suitable for their child
    D   Poorly geriatrics

49. No one over 18 is allowed to see a film with an 18 classification. True or false?

50. Which of the following statements is correct?

A If you have a television licence, you can have a TV is every room of the house.
B If you have more than one television, you must have a licence for each one.

51. Can youngsters aged 16 or 17 drink alcohol in a public place?

A No, they cannot drink alcohol anywhere until they're 18
B Yes, they can drink alcohol as long as they're with an adult
C Yes, they can drink alcohol but only on the street
D Yes, but only wine or beer, and they must drink it with a meal in a hotel or restaurant

52 What must the collars of all dogs in public places show?

A The dog's name
B Any allergies the dog has
C The owner's name and address
D The dog's breed and age

53. If your dog makes a mess on the pavement, no one will mind if you don't clean it up. True or false?

54. What do you need to travel on public transport in the UK?

A A timetable
B A ticket
C A map
D An umbrella

55. What's the difference between a black cab and a minicab?

A Black cabs are black and minicabs must be another colour
B Black cabs are used in London, while minicabs are used elsewhere
C Black cabs are licensed but minicabs aren't
D Black cabs are a traditional type of taxi, while minicabs are cars which are used as taxis

56. What's the first step towards getting a full driving licence?

A Learning to drive
B Buying a car
C Taking a driving test
D Applying for a provisional licence

57. **For your car to be legal on UK roads, you must have which four documents?**

A   A driving licence, insurance certificate, your passport and a receipt for the purchase of the car
B   A driving licence, a road tax disc, an insurance certificate and an MOT certificate
C   A road tax disc, a provisional driving licence, L plates and an MOT certificate
D   A driving licence, a utility bill, an MOT certificate and a road tax disc

58. **No one in the UK is allowed to ride a motorcycle without wearing a crash helmet. True or false?**

59. **What should you do if you have a minor road accident? p**

A   Drive away as fast as possible
B   Apologise to the other driver
C   Exchange names, addresses and insurance details with the other driver
D   Dial 999

60. **What is the government planning to introduce in the next few years?**

A   Free Easter eggs for every child
B   Identity cards
C   The Euro
D   Cat licences

The answers are on page 205.

Gherkin building, City of London

6.

EMPLOYMENT

This chapter is all about the world of work. It explains how to look for and apply for jobs, with tips on how to be successful; it also covers options for training and volunteering, which will boost your job prospects. We also look at how employers should treat you, as well as your rights and responsibilities at work, and how to go about working for yourself. Finally, it provides information about childcare and the regulations regarding children at work.

FINDING A JOB

There are many work opportunities in the UK, which is one of the reasons so many immigrants want to live there. Applying for a job can be a complicated process, but there's a lot of help and information available, and UK workers are well protected by the law.

Are You Permitted to Work in the UK?

Not everyone in the UK is allowed to work; some people need work permits, while others aren't permitted to work at all – which should be stated in your visa stamp. Employers must make sure that anyone they employ is legally entitled (has the right) to work in the UK, therefore it's important to check your status before applying for a job.

The Home Office provides guidance and information about who is (and isn't) allowed to work in Britain – see the Working in the UK website (🖳 www.workingintheuk.gov.uk).

Resources for Jobseekers

There are a number of ways to go about finding work in the UK and many places you can look for employment.

♦ Advertisements in the jobs sections of newspapers (local and national).

♦ Employment agencies – these include private agencies and Jobcentre Plus (see below).

♦ The internet – check the websites of companies or organisations you would like to work for, as most advertise their vacancies online. All the major recruitment agencies (companies which match employees with the right job) also have websites.

♦ Supermarket notice boards and shop windows – but remember that many of these vacancies are part-time and wages can be low.

Jobcentre Plus

Jobcentre Plus is a government agency run by the Department for Work and Pensions, which has branches throughout the UK. You can find the name and address of the one nearest to you under 'Jobcentre Plus' in the phone book, or by visiting their website (💻 www. jobcentreplus.gov.uk).

Jobcentres have trained staff who can advise on finding and applying for jobs, and also help with claiming benefits and arrange an interpreter. The Jobcentre Plus website lists vacancies and training opportunities, and provides general information on benefits (💻 www. jobcentreplus.gov.uk).

For advice and job information by phone, call Jobseeker Direct (☎ 0845-60 60 234, 9am to 6pm weekdays, 9am to 1pm Saturdays).

Qualifications

Some jobs require applicants to have special training or qualifications, such as a diploma or certificate. If you have qualifications which were gained in another country, you must find out how they compare with those awarded in the UK by contacting the National Academic Recognition Information Centre (UK NARIC, ECCTIS Ltd, Oriel House, Oriel Road, Cheltenham Glos., GL50 1XP, ☎ 0870-990 4088, 💻 www.naric.org.uk).

Job Applications

How you apply for a job depends on the type of job. If it's something local and low paid, you can probably arrange an interview in person or over the phone. However, for many jobs it's necessary to complete an application form or send a copy of your curriculum vitae (CV – see below) with a covering letter or a letter of application. Employers will then use this information to decide whether or not to interview you.

- How to check whether you can work legally in the UK.
- The places where jobs are advertised.
- All about Jobcentre Plus and Jobseeker Direct.
- How to check if your overseas qualifications are accepted in the UK.

Letters & CVs

A covering letter is one which you attach to a completed application form. If you need to provide more details about why you're applying for a job and why you think you're suitable, you should write a longer letter of application. Always include your contact details such as address, telephone number and an email address (if you have one).

Your CV (resumé) is a short history of your working life – it should include details about your education and qualifications, your previous jobs, plus any relevant skills and interests. If you're completing an application form, you may not need to include a CV. Be honest about your skills and qualifications as employers can check these facts.

Make sure that you type your CV and any letters on a computer or word processor: this makes a good impression, ensures that employers don't have to struggle to read your handwriting and will give you a better chance of getting an interview.

Advice on handling job application forms, writing a covering letter and CV, and preparing for job interviews is available from Jobcentre Plus.

Referees

Job applicants are often asked to provide details of two referees. These are people who know you well and also know your skills and work history, for example a previous employer or a college tutor. Employers will ask them to confirm your suitability for the job that you're applying for, by writing a short report or reference. Family and friends aren't acceptable as referees.

Interviews

Sooner or later, you will need to attend a job interview where the potential employer will ask you to expand on the information provided in your initial application. It's important to give honest answers to the interviewer, especially about your qualifications and past experience. If an employer discovers that you gave false (incorrect) information, you could lose the job.

As well as 'selling' yourself to the employer, interviews are also an opportunity to learn what the job involves, including details such as the salary, annual holidays and working conditions. Ask, too, about the organisation – employers like candidates who show interest – and do some research so that you can talk about the company as well as yourself.

Popular areas of questioning in interviews include:

♦ Why you want to work for the organisation or company.

♦ Your responsibilities in your current and past jobs.

♦ Why you left, or are leaving, your current job.

♦ What you see yourself doing in five years' time.

must know

↻ How to write and present a covering letter and CV.

↻ What a referee is and what they do.

↻ What to expect at a job interview.

↻ What a Criminal Records Bureau (CRB) check is, and who might need one.

Criminal Record

Some jobs, especially those which involve contact with children or vulnerable people – for example, working as a teaching assistant or looking after elderly people – require employers to check your criminal record before they can confirm a job offer. They must ask your permission before they can do this.

For more information about criminal record checks, contact the Home Office Criminal Records Bureau (☎ 0870-909 0811) or, in Scotland, Disclosure Scotland (☎ 0870-609 6006, 🖥 www.disclosurescotland.co.uk).

Training

Training for extra qualifications increases your chances of finding a good job. A good example is English language training, although there are many skills-based courses available. Some employers provide 'on the job' training (while you work) or you can take a course at a local college or from home. For more information, contact your local college, visit the library or see training-based websites such as 🖥 www.worktrain.gov.uk and 🖥 www.learndirect.co.uk

Learndirect offers online courses (where you train via the internet) at centres throughout the UK. You must pay for courses but can do a free starter or test session to see whether it's the right course for you. For more information, call Learndirect's information line (☎ 0800-100900).

Volunteering & Work Experience

Voluntary work is unpaid but is a good way to gain experience while supporting your local community. A lot of organisations depend on the help of volunteers, such as animal charities and groups which look after the environment; being a volunteer looks good on your CV and will improve your job prospects. Your library will have information about ways and places where you can volunteer and there are also many websites (🖥 www.do-it.org.uk, 🖥 www.volunteering.org.uk and 🖥 www.justdosomething.net).

Work experience is working for an employer to gain experience rather than wages. You join a company or organisation for a short period of time to learn about a job and/or industry – prospective employers like to see that an applicant has done work experience in their industry.

must know

- ↻ The different types of training available and where to learn about them.

- ↻ Why volunteering and work experience are good for your job prospects.

EQUAL RIGHTS & DISCRIMINATION

Under UK law, employers cannot discriminate against someone at work. This means that it's against the law to refuse someone work, training or promotion (gaining a better job in the same organisation), or treat them less favourably, due to any of the following:

- ◆ sex or gender;

- ◆ nationality, race, colour or ethnic group;

- ◆ disability;

- ◆ religion;

- ◆ sexual orientation, e.g. no one should be discriminated against for being homosexual;

- ◆ age;

- ◆ religious beliefs or political opinions.

UK law supports equal rights for men and women: if both sexes do the same job or work of equal value, they should receive equal pay. Almost all the laws which protect people at work apply equally, whether you're doing full- or part-time work. There are only a small number of jobs to which discrimination laws don't apply, e.g. if a job involves an employee working for someone in their own home, then discrimination isn't against the law.

The Citizens Advice Bureau has information about the laws that protect people at work (🖥 www.adviceguide.org.uk). In addition, there are a number of organisations that provide information and advice about discrimination, which can also, in certain situations, support the claims of individuals who feel they've been discriminated against:

◆ Racial discrimination – the Commission for Racial Equality;

◆ Sex discrimination – the Equal Opportunities Commission;

◆ Disability discrimination – the Disability Rights Commission.

From October 2007, the three organisations listed above have been combined into a new Commission for Equality and Human Rights (🖥 www.equalityhumanrights.com).

Northern Ireland has its own Equality Commission, which provides information and advice about all forms of illegal discrimination. It can be contacted at The Equality Commission for Northern Ireland, Equality House, 7-9 Shaftesbury Square, Belfast BT2 7DP (☎ 028-9050 0600, 🖥 www.equalityni.org).

Sexual Harassment

Sexual harassment (unwelcome advances or comments of a sexual nature) is often thought to be a problem affecting women, but both sexes can experience sexual harassment at work, and it can take a number of different forms, such as:

◆ inappropriate (not proper) touching or sexual demands;

◆ indecent (offensive) remarks;

◆ comments or questions about your sex life;

◆ comments about the way you look, which makes you feel uncomfortable or humiliated (losing pride);

◆ bullying (intimidating) behaviour, or being treated in a way which is rude, hostile, degrading, or humiliating because of your sex.

What should you do if this happens to you? Don't keep quiet about it, but ask the person harassing you to stop, and tell a work colleague or friend about what is happening. If you're a member of a trade union, inform your union representative. It's also advisable to keep a written record which includes what happened, the dates and times, and details of any witnesses who may have seen or heard what happened.

If the problem persists, report the person to your employer and your trade union. Employers are responsible for the way their employees behave at work, and should take any complaints about sexual harassment very seriously and take action to deal with them. If your employer doesn't take appropriate action (and sometimes it's your boss who is doing the harassing), you can take your case to the Equal Opportunities Commission (or the new Commission for Equality and Human Rights), as well as to your trade union or a Citizens Advice Bureau.

- What is meant by discrimination and the types of discrimination which can occur
- That there are laws against discrimination, especially in the workplace, but there are exceptions to those laws.
- That men and women have equal rights to a job and salary, regardless of their gender.
- The different commissions set up to combat discrimination.
- What sexual harassment is, the forms it can take and what to do if it happens to you.
- Employers' responsibility for dealing with sexual harassment among their workers.

RESPONSIBILITIES AT WORK

In the workplace, both employer and employee have legal responsibilities, and each must make sure that they fulfil these requirements.

Employers must:

- ◆ treat their employees fairly;
- ◆ be responsible for their health and safety;
- ◆ pay them for the work they do.

Employees must:

- ◆ follow their employer's instructions;
- ◆ do their work with reasonable skill and care;
- ◆ take care not to damage their employer's business.

A Written Contract or Statement

Your contract or statement of employment is an important document which sets out the details and conditions of your job, and should include the following:

- your responsibilities at work;

- how much you're paid;

- your working hours;

- the amount of holiday you can take;

- your entitlement to sick pay (payment when you're off work sick);

- details of your pension, if your employer provides one;

- how many days' notice (warning) both you and your employer should give before employment can be terminated.

You should receive your contract or statement of employment within two months of starting a job. Don't lose it, as it's an important document, particularly if you have a disagreement with your boss over your work, pay or other conditions.

Pay, Hours & Holidays

How much you're paid is something that you agree with your employer. He or she must pay you at least the minimum wage, which is a legal right for every employee aged above the compulsory school-leaving age. No one can leave school before the age of 16 – the actual time in the school year when a 16 year old can leave is different in England and Wales from that in Scotland and Northern Ireland – but as soon as anyone leaves school the minimum wage rules apply.

The minimum wage depends on your age; the older you are, the higher it is. The rates from October 2006 were as follows:

- workers aged 22 or older   £5.35 an hour

- 18 – 21-year-olds   £4.45 an hour

- 16 – 17-year-olds   £3.30 an hour

If you're paid less than the minimum wage for your age, then your employer is breaking the law. If this happens to you, you should contact the Minimum Wage Helpline (☎ 0845-600 0678). You can obtain more information about the minimum wage from the Central Office of Information's Directgov website (🖳 www.direct.gov.uk), which provides a lot of public service information about everything from employment and tax to health and transport.

Each time you're paid, your employer should provide a statement in writing, such as a pay slip, which shows how much you've been paid and how much money has been deducted (taken away) for income tax and National Insurance (see below).

Time Off

Just as there's a minimum wage, there's also a minimum holiday entitlement: all employees must get at least four weeks' paid holiday a year. This includes time taken off for national public holidays (see **Public Holidays** on page 53). You may need to be absent (away) from work if you're ill or have a medical appointment, and should inform your employer as soon as you can – first thing in the morning if you're ill, or as soon as your appointment is made.

The hours you work should be shown in your contract or statement of employment. Your employer may ask you to work extra hours, and it's up to you whether you agree to or not, but an employer cannot force you to work more hours than those stated in your contract.

Tax

If you're employed, then your income tax payments should be deducted automatically from your wages by your employer and paid to the government. If you're self-employed (work for yourself) you must pay your own tax (see **Working for Yourself** on page 157). Money raised through income tax pays for government services, such as:

♦ the armed forces (army, navy and air force);

♦ the police service;

♦ education;

♦ roads.

Tax is collected by HM Revenue and Customs.Sometimes they require more details about an individual's finances, and will send out a form called a tax return. If you receive one you must complete it and return it as soon as possible, as it will affect the amount of tax you pay.

For help and advice about completing a tax return, contact HM Revenue and Customs self-assessment helpline (☎ 0845-300 4555).

must know

- ♂ The responsibilities of both employers and employees.

- ♂ What should be included in a contract or statement of employment, and when you should receive one.

- ♂ The legal minimum wage for different age groups, which employers must pay.

- ♂ What a pay slip should include.

- ♂ The legal minimum holiday entitlement.

- ♂ Who decides how many hours you work.

National Insurance

Almost everyone working in the UK – including self-employed people – must pay National Insurance (NI) contributions, which are deducted by your employer in the same way as income tax. Money collected from NI payments goes towards the welfare benefits system, in particular the State Retirement Pension (see Pensions on page 153) and the National Health Service.

If you're self-employed, you must pay your NI contributions (NICs) yourself. There are two separate payments:

♦ Class 2 NICs are paid as a regular payment, either every three months or by direct debit.

♦ Class 4 NICs are calculated on the profits from your trade or business, and paid at the same time as you pay your income tax.

If you don't pay sufficient NI contributions, you won't be able to claim certain benefits such as Jobseeker's Allowance or Maternity Pay. More importantly, you may not qualify for a full State Retirement Pension.

Getting a National Insurance Number

In order to work in the UK, you need a National Insurance (NI) number. This is a unique (one-off) number which tracks your National Insurance contributions. Citizens receive their number just before their 16th birthday, but immigrants who are eligible to work in the UK need to apply for one. You can do this through your local Jobcentre Plus or Social Security Office, and should phone to make an appointment and check the documents that you will need to take along – usually your birth certificate, passport and/or Home Office documents permitting you to stay in the UK.

Refugees who've been successful in applying for asylum have the same rights to work as any other British citizen and should receive an NI number, but those who've applied for asylum and not yet received a decision must wait – they cannot work or apply for an NI number until asylum has been granted.

For more information about registering for a national insurance number, contact the National Insurance Registrations Helpline (☎ 0845-915 7006 or 0845-915 5670).

Pensions

Everyone who has paid enough National Insurance contributions will receive a State Pension when they retire (stop working). The age you can retire and receive the state pension depends on whether you're male or female and when you were born:

♦ Men can receive the State Pension from the age of 65.

♦ Women can receive a State Pension from the age of 60. However, the retirement age for women is changing so that it matches that of men – equality works both ways – so the State Pension retirement age for women will increase to 65, in stages between 2010 and 2020.

For more information about the State Pension scheme, contact the Pension Service (☎ 0845-606 0265, 🖳 www.thepensionservice.gov.uk).

Private Pensions

The State Pension doesn't pay a great deal of money, therefore people can choose to top it up by contributing to other pension schemes. Many receive a pension through their employer, called an occupational pension, and some also have private pension plans. Pensions are a large investment for your future, and it pays to obtain good advice before investing in one, from:

♦ The Pensions Advisory Service (☎ 0845-601 2923, 🖳 www.opas.org.uk) provides free and confidential advice about both occupational and private pensions.

♦ Independent financial advisors (IFAs) – as with a solicitor or accountant, you can consult an IFA but must pay for their advice. You can find IFAs in the Yellow Pages or Thomson local guide, or visit 🖳 www.unbiased.co.uk.

⌒ That everyone who works in the UK must pay income tax and National Insurance contributions.

⌒ How your income tax is collected and what it pays for.

⌒ What a tax return is.

⌒ What National Insurance (NI) is, and what it pays for.

⌒ The NI contributions which self-employed people must make.

⌒ How you might miss out if you don't pay enough NICs.

⌒ The age at which men and women can receive a State Pension, and how this is changing.

⌒ What occupational and private pensions are, and how to obtain advice about them.

Health & Safety

Both employers and employees must follow health and safety rules at work. Employers have a legal duty to make sure that their workplace is safe, while employees have a legal duty to follow safety regulations and to work in a safe and responsible way. If you're concerned about health and safety at work, don't ignore a problem, as your boss needs to know. Talk to your supervisor, manager or trade union representative, who should know the right procedure to follow in order to make a report. You cannot be dismissed or unfairly treated by your employer for raising concerns about health and safety, and you may even save someone's life.

Trade Unions

Trade unions are organisations which are made up of (and work for) employees. They aim to improve the working conditions and pay for their members, which they may do by organising a strike, which is when workers refuse to do their job unless management is willing to listen to their demands. However, they also provide useful advice, and support members who have problems at work. Most trade unions represent a particular industry or employment sector. You can decide whether or not to join a union, and your employer cannot dismiss you from your job, or treat you unfairly, for being a union member – or for not being one.

The Trades Union Congress (TUC, 🖳 www.tuc.org.uk) is an umbrella organisation whose members include all the UK's trade unions. It can provide details about the different unions, as well as the benefits they offer to workers and information regarding your rights in the workplace.

Problems at Work

Sometimes things go wrong at work, so who can you turn to for advice? You should start by talking to someone in a position of authority, such as your supervisor or manager. Take advice before you take any action: if you're a trade union member your union representative should be able to help. You can also obtain help from a local Citizens Advice Bureau or Law Centre, and the Advisory, Conciliation and Arbitration Service (ACAS, ☎ 0845-747 4747, 🖥 www.acas.org.uk), a national organisation which can advise you about your rights at work.

must know

❂ The role of employers and employees in workplace health and safety.

❂ What to do if you have concerns about health and safety.

❂ What a trade union is and how it can help you.

❂ That all workers have the right to join a trade union.

❂ How to deal with problems at work.

Losing Your Job & Unfair Dismissal

It's difficult to fire someone from their job in the UK, unless they're guilty of serious misconduct (wrongdoing), such as theft or sexual harassment or violence against another employee, which are all grounds for immediate dismissal. However, in most cases an employer will issue an employee with a warning for unsatisfactory behaviour, which might include being frequently absent from work, repeatedly showing up late and not doing their job properly. If an employee's attendance, punctuality (being on time) and work doesn't improve, the employer can give a worker notice to terminate his employment.

An employer cannot dismiss someone from work unfairly, e.g. for one of the reasons listed under **Equal Rights & Discrimination** (see page 148), which is called unfair dismissal. If this happens to you, or your working life is made so difficult that you feel you have no choice but to leave, then you can take your case to an Employment Tribunal, which is a special 'court' that examines matters of employment. You have three months in which to make a complaint of unfair dismissal, but it's worthwhile doing so, because if you win the case you may receive compensation.

If you lose your job, you should obtain advice regarding your legal rights and the best action to take, as soon as possible, by talking to:

♦ your trade union representative;

♦ a solicitor;

♦ a Law Centre;

♦ a Citizens Advice Bureau.

Redundancy

Redundancy is when you lose your job because your employer can no longer afford to employ you, or no longer needs someone to do your job. It isn't because you're bad at your job, and you may be entitled to redundancy pay: a one off payment to compensate you for losing your job. The amount you receive depends on the amount of time you've been employed by the company, but redundancy payments can be generous.

If you're being made redundant, you can seek advice from the same sources as you would if you lost your job or were unfairly dismissed: your trade union representative, a solicitor, a Law Centre or a Citizens Advice Bureau.

Unemployment

Unemployment occurs when you're able to work but cannot find a job. The government can help by paying you some money while you look for work: there's a welfare benefit called Jobseeker's Allowance (JSA) which can be paid to men aged 18 to 65 and women aged 18 to 60 who are able to work and are looking for a job. Young people aged 16 and 17 may be able to claim a Young Person's Bridging Allowance (YPBA).

For help on claims, visit your nearest Jobcentre Plus (🖥 www.jobcentreplus.gov.uk) or contact a Citizens Advice Bureau.

must know

- Reasons why an employee might lose his job.

- What help is available if you lose your job – and the time you have to make a complaint.

- What happens at an Employment Tribunal.

- The difference between unfair dismissal and redundancy.

- How the government helps unemployed people.

- What the New Deal is and who it applies to.

New Deal

New Deal is a government-run programme to help the long-term unemployed. Young people who've been out of work for six months and adults who've been out of work for 18 months must join New Deal if they wish to continue receiving unemployment benefits. In return, they're provided with extra help and support to find employment – there are different schemes for different age groups. If they choose not to join New Deal, they may lose their benefit payments.

There's also a work-based learning programme which offers extra training to people in work. They're able to earn while they learn, as they're paid a wage or allowance, but have time off work to attend college and gain qualifications. For information, contact New Deal (☎ 0845-606 2626, 🖥 www.newdeal.gov.uk).

For advice about other government schemes in your area, see the Jobcentre Plus website (🖥 www.jobcentreplus.gov.uk) or visit a Citizens Advice Bureau.

WORKING FOR YOURSELF

Many people in the UK choose to be self-employed (work for themselves). There are many opportunities, but working for yourself also brings extra responsibilities, such as paying your own tax and National Insurance contributions.

Tax

As soon as you become self-employed, you must register for tax and National Insurance with HM Revenue and Customs. Self-employed people must keep a careful record of everything they earn and spend on their business. Business accounts must be sent to HM Revenue and Customs each year, and tax payments are calculated from these accounts. Many people employ an accountant to make sure that they pay the correct amount of tax and they claim all their tax allowances. For information about self-employed National Insurance contributions, see **National Insurance** on page 152. HM Revenue and Customs has a useful helpline for the self-employed (☎ 0845- 915 4515).

That self-employed people must keep accounts and pay their own tax and NICs.

Where to get help if you're self-employed.

What Business Link can do for you.

That British citizens can also work in EEA countries.

Help & Advice

There is help and advice available for people who decide to work for themselves. Banks can advise about setting up a business and may offer start-up loans, although they charge interest on the repayments, therefore you need to budget for the extra money to cover this.

Business Link (☎ 0845-600 9006, 🖥 www. businesslink.gov.uk) is a government-funded organisation that provides advice about grants and loans available to the newly self-employed, as well as providing more general advice.

Working in Europe

British citizens aren't limited to working in the UK. They can seek employment in any country which is a member state of the European Economic Area (EEA), and should have the same employment rights as a citizen of that country.

CHILDCARE & CHILDREN AT WORK

The UK government provides help for new parents so that they can take time off work to look after a baby, as well as rules to safeguard children with part-time jobs.

New Mothers & Fathers

Mothers: all women who are employed, either full-time or part-time, are entitled to take at least 26 weeks off work when they're pregnant and after the baby is born, which is called maternity leave. It doesn't matter how long a woman has worked for her employer, she's still entitled to maternity leave, but it's important to follow the correct procedures and let the employer know about the pregnancy as soon as possible. Some women are also entitled to payment during maternity leave – called maternity pay – but this depends on how long she's worked for her employer.

Fathers: men who've worked for their employer for at least 26 weeks can take time off to care for a new baby, which is called paternity leave. They receive up to two weeks' paid leave, but as with mums-to-be, must inform their employer as soon as possible.

For more advice and information about maternity and paternity allowances, contact:

♦ your personnel officer at work;

♦ your trade union representative;

♦ a Citizens Advice Bureau (💻 www. adviceguide.org.uk);

♦ the Directgov website (💻 www.direct.gov.uk).

Childcare

The UK government helps parents with childcare so that they can return to work, and some employers also provide assistance. ChildcareLink (☎ 0800-234 6346, 💻 www.childcarelink. gov.uk) provides information about childcare options, as well as listing registered childminders (people who can look after your children) in your area.

Children at Work

Many children in the UK have part-time jobs to earn pocket money or help out their family; however, there are strict rules about the employment of children to ensure that work doesn't get in the way of their education and that they're not exploited. It's necessary for children aged below the school-leaving age (17) to obtain a permit to work from the local authority.

The youngest age that a child can legally work is 13, although there are exceptions for some types of work, such as modelling or acting. Children taking part in some kind of performance, such as acting in a film, need a medical certificate, as well as a local authority permit, before they can start work.

♻ The minimum entitlement for maternity leave for full-time and part-time workers – and who gets maternity pay.

♻ How long a man must work before he can take paid paternity leave.

♻ How the government helps with childcare.

Children under 16 can only do certain types of light work. Jobs they aren't permitted to do include:

♦ delivering milk;

♦ working in a kitchen;

♦ working in a fish and chip shop;

♦ working with heavy machinery or chemicals;

♦ selling medication, alcohol or cigarettes;

♦ doing any work which might harm their health or education.

There are also rules about the amount of time and the hours that children can work. Those aged 13 to 16 must have at least two consecutive weeks a year (i.e. a full fortnight) during school holidays when they don't work. In addition, they must not work:

♦ more than four hours without a one-hour break;

♦ more than two hours on any school day or Sunday;

♦ for more than five hours (13 to 14-year-olds) or eight hours (15 to 16-year-olds) on a Saturday or a weekday during the school holidays;

♦ before 7am or after 7pm;

♦ before school closes for the day, although in some areas children can work for an hour before school;

♦ for more than 12 hours in any school week;

♦ for more than 25 hours a week (13 to 14-year-olds) or 35 hours a week (15 to 16-years-olds) during school holidays.

If a child works for longer than he or she should, the local authority may withdraw their licence to work and they would then have to stop working. In addition, their parents and employers could face prosecution. There's no minimum wage for children under 16.

♦ An employer can be prosecuted for illegally employing a child.

♦ Parents and carers may be prosecuted for making a false declaration on a child's work licence application, and for not making sure that a child attends school.

For more information visit the TUC website (💻 www.worksmart.org.uk).

must know

!

⟳ The minimum age at which children can legally start work – and the exceptions

⟳ When licences and medical certificates are required.

⟳ How the local authority is involved in children working.

⟳ The responsibilities of parents, carers and employers.

⟳ Jobs which children cannot legally do.

⟳ The restrictions on the hours children can work.

WORDS TO LEARN

Check that you understand this chapter's key terms:

Looking for Work

work permit
permitted, entitled
advertisements
employment agency, recruitment agency
Jobcentre Plus, Jobseeker Direct
qualification(s)
application form
curriculum vitae (CV)
covering letter
reference, referee
interview, candidate
vulnerable
criminal record, Criminal Records Bureau (CRB)
training, Learndirect
voluntary work, volunteering
work experience

Equal Rights & Discrimination

discrimination
equal rights
promotion
full-time work, part-time work
racial discrimination, sexual discrimination, disability discrimination
sexual harassment
inappropriate, indecent
humiliating, bullying, degrading

At Work

contract/statement of employment
sick pay
minimum wage
pay slip, deduction
holiday entitlement
income tax
HM Revenue and Customs
self-employed
National Insurance (NI), National Insurance contributions (NICs)
National Insurance number
refugee, asylum
retire, retirement age
State Pension
occupational pension, private pension
independent financial advisor (IFA)
health and safety
trade union, union member, Trades Union Congress
serious misconduct
attendance, punctuality
unfair dismissal

Employment Tribunal
redundancy, redundancy pay
unemployment
Jobseeker's Allowance (JSA)
New Deal

Working for Yourself

self-employed
business accounts
accountant

tax allowances
start-up loan

Childcare & Children at Work

maternity leave, maternity pay
paternity leave
registered childminder
medical certificate
consecutive

PRACTICE QUESTIONS

Now test your knowledge of employment with these practice questions. Make sure that you can answer them all before you take your test.

1. **Which government department advises on who is legally entitled to work in Britain?**

   A   The Department for Work and Pensions
   B   The Home Office
   C   The Foreign and Commonwealth Office
   D   The Labour Party

2. **Where should you look for a job if you want to work for a particular UK company or organisation?**

   A   Supermarket notice boards
   B   Local newspapers
   C   The company's website
   D   Jobcentre Plus

3. **What is Jobcentre Plus?**

   A   A government agency that advises on finding work and claiming benefits
   B   A private employment agency
   C   A jobseekers' newspaper
   D   A recruitment website

4. **Where can you check how qualifications gained abroad compare with UK qualifications?**

   A   The Home Office
   B   Any employment agency
   C   The Citizens Advice Bureau
   D   The National Academic Recognition Information Centre

5. **What might you need to supply when applying for a job? Give two answers.**

   A   A stamped addressed envelope
   B   A covering letter
   C   A copy of your CV
   D   Your driving licence

6. **Friends and relatives aren't generally accepted as a job candidate's referees. True or false.**

7. **What are the possible consequences of telling lies during a job interview?**

    A   You may be sacked later
    B   You may be promoted later
    C   You may be deported later
    D   You may be arrested later

8. **Which of the following statements is correct?**

    A   Employers like people who ask a lot of questions at a job interview
    B   People who don't ask questions at a job interview are more likely to get the job

9. **Which type of jobs might require an applicant to undergo a Criminal Records Bureau check? Give two answers.**

    A   Those which involve working with animals
    B   Those that involve working with elderly people
    C   Those that involve working with children
    D   Those that involve working with members of the opposite sex

10. **Why is it a good idea to do voluntary work?**

    A   It's very well paid
    B   It leads to extra qualifications
    C   It gives you extra experience and looks good on your CV
    D   It's the only work available to immigrants

11. **In general, on what grounds may an employer discriminate against an employee?**

    A   Their age
    B   Their gender
    C   Their religion
    D   None of the above

12. **It's illegal to discriminate against people because they're overweight or have bad personal hygiene. True or false?**

13. **In which of the following circumstances do the discrimination laws not apply?**

    A   When the job involves working with young people
    B   When the job involves working in the employer's home
    C   When an individual has more than one disability
    D   When it's a part-time job

14. **It's illegal in Northern Ireland to discriminate against someone because of their political opinions. True or false?**

15. **Which of the following could be classed as sexual harassment?**

    A   Asking someone when they last had sex
    B   Touching someone's thigh
    C   Telling someone they look fat and undesirable
    D   All of the above

16. **Which of the following should you do if you think you're being sexually harassed? Give two answers.**

    A   Tell your employer, colleague, trade union representative or friend
    B   Leave your job
    C   Call the police
    D   Keep notes of what happens and when

17. **Which of the following statements is correct?**

    A   Employers need only take action when female workers are being sexually harassed
    B   If male employees are sexually harassed it's important that employees take action

18. **When should a man and woman receive equal pay?**

    A   When they're doing the same job
    B   When they work in the same department
    C   When they're the same age
    D   When they're both members of a trade union

19. **What should you have received within two months of starting a new job?**

    A   A pay rise
    B   A contract of employment
    C   A uniform
    D   A promotion

20. **Which of the following should be included in a statement of employment? Give two answers.**

    A   How much you earn
    B   How many qualifications you have
    C   How many days' holiday you can take
    D   How much tax you pay

21. **What is the minimum wage for workers aged over 22?**

    A £4.45 per hour
    B £3.30 per hour
    C £5.35 per hour
    D £6.50 per hour

22. **Which of the following statements is correct?**

    A All employees are entitled to at least four weeks' holiday a year, plus national public holidays
    B All employees are entitled to at least four weeks' holiday a year, including national public holidays

23. **How many more hours than stated on an individual's contract can their employer force them to work?**

    A Ten hours a week
    B One hour a day
    C None
    D As many as they like

24. **What type of tax is taken automatically from an individual's earnings?**

    A Road tax
    B Income tax
    C Council tax
    D Employment tax

25. **Which of the following government expenses does income tax go towards paying? Give two answers.**

    A The State Pension
    B The National Health Service
    C The army
    D Education

26. **If you don't complete a tax return you don't need to pay any tax. True or false?**

27. **Which government department is responsible for collecting tax?**

    A The Home Office
    B HM Revenue and Customs
    C The Department of Work and Pensions
    D The National Insurance department

28. Who pays Class 2 and Class 4 NICs?

A   Everyone
B   People over 60
C   Unemployed people
D   Self-employed people

29. Which of the following may be ineligible for Maternity Pay and Jobseekers' Allowance?

A   Women who are already receiving benefits
B   Women who haven't made sufficient National Insurance contributions
C   Women over 50
D   Any woman that's already had a baby

30. When do British citizens receive their National Insurance number?

A   When they're born
B   When they leave school
C   Just before the 16th birthday
D   Just before they start work

31. Which of the following statements is correct?

A   Refugees who've applied for asylum cannot work or apply for an NI number until it's granted
B   Refugees who've applied for asylum can work and apply for an NI number while waiting for a decision on their application

32. Where do you apply for a National Insurance number? Give two answers.

A   The post office
B   HM Revenue and Customs
C   Jobcentre Plus
D   Social Security office

33. Which document might you need when applying for a national insurance number?

A   Your contract of employment
B   Your CV
C   Your tax return
D   Your passport

34. **If you don't pay sufficient National Insurance contributions, which benefits might you miss out on?**

    A   Maternity Pay
    B   Jobseeker's Allowance
    C   The full amount of the State Pension
    D   All of the above

35. **Both men and women are eligible to receive a State Pension at the same age. True or false?**

36. **Where can you obtain advice about occupational and private pensions? Give two answers.**

    A   An independent financial advisor
    B   The Pension Service
    C   The Pensions Advisory Service
    D   HM Revenue and Customs

37. **Who is responsible for following health and safety rules in the workplace?**

    A   Employers
    B   Employees
    C   Both of the above
    D   The government

38. **What do trade unions do?**

    A   Lend money to their members
    B   Organise and work on behalf of employers
    C   Work to improve international trade
    D   Work to improve working conditions and pay for their members

39. **Which of the following statements is correct?**

    A   You must join a trade union, even if your employer threatens to dismiss you from your job
    B   You can decide whether or not to join a union, and your employer cannot dismiss you from your job for being a union member

40. **Which of the following might cause an employer to serve you with a warning? Give two answers.**

    A   Poor dress sense
    B   Bad time-keeping
    C   Asking for more money
    D   Not doing your job properly

41. How long do you normally have to take a complaint of unfair dismissal to an Employment Tribunal?

A   Three weeks
B   Three months
C   Three years
D   There's no time limit

42. What is redundancy? Give two answers.

A   When you decide to leave your job and give your employer notice
B   When your employer dismisses you because he cannot afford to employ you
C   When you have to leave work because your job is no longer needed
D   When you're forced to leave a job due to serious misconduct

43. If your employer makes you redundant, you cannot take him to an Employment Tribunal. True or false?

44. Who is entitled to a Young Person's Bridging Allowance?

A   16 and 17-year-olds who are going into further education
B   16 and 17-year-olds who are entering the construction industry
C   16 and 17-year-olds who are unemployed
D   16 and 17-year-olds who've just had a baby

45. Young people who've been unemployed for six months and adults who've been unemployed for 18 months, are encouraged to join which government scheme?

A   New Start
B   New Deal
C   Deal or No Deal
D   New Chance

46. What do lots of self-employed people use to make sure they pay their taxes correctly?

A   An accountant
B   Their bank manager
C   Jobcentre Plus
D   An independent financial advisor

47. What must you do as soon as you become self-employed?

A   Inform HM Revenue and Customs
B   Inform the Home Office
C   Inform your nearest Jobcentre Plus\
D   Inform your family

48. If you work for yourself, you pay income tax once a month. True or false?

49. What is the name of the organisation that advises people about starting and running a business?

    A   Business News
    B   Business Link
    C   Business Advice
    D   Business World

50. Where are British citizens not allowed to work without a work permit?

    A   Ireland
    B   France
    C   Anywhere in the United States of America
    D   Anywhere in the European Economic Area

51. Expectant women are entitled to how much maternity leave?

    A   At least 52 weeks
    B   At least 26 weeks
    C   At least 12 weeks
    D   At least 36 weeks

52. How long must a man work for an employer in order to be entitled to paternity pay?

    A   At least 26 weeks
    B   At least a month
    C   At least 52 weeks
    D   At least 17 weeks

53. How much time off work can a new father take?

    A   Up to 26 weeks
    B   Up to six months
    C   Up to two weeks
    D   Up to a month

54. Can children work before they are aged 14?

    A   No, not at all
    B   Yes, they can do any job they like
    C   Only if their parents agree
    D   Yes, but only in certain trades and only if the relevant licences and medical certificates are obtained

55. **Which of the following jobs are children aged between 14 and 16 legally permitted to do?**

    A   Working in a fish and chip shop
    B   Working in an off licence
    C   Delivering newspapers
    D   Delivering milk

56. **Children are allowed to work as performers provided they have a local authority licence and medical certificate. True or false?**

57. **How many consecutive weeks in school holidays must 14 to 16-year-olds take off from work?**

    A   Three
    B   Two
    C   Four
    D   The entire holiday period

58. **Between what hours is a 15-year-old allowed to work?**

    A   7pm and 7am
    B   9am and 5pm
    C   5pm and 9am
    D   7am and 7pm

59. **Which of the following statements is true?**

    A   A 14-year-old who works must take a one hour break every four hours
    B   A 14-year-old who works may only work for one hour in every four

60. **What could a local authority do if they think a child is working illegally? Give two answers.**

    A   Make sure they get fired
    B   Withdraw their licence so they can no longer work
    C   Ensure they get a bonus
    D   Prosecute the employer

The answers are on page 206.

7.

AFTER THE TEST

You've passed the Life in the UK test – well done! So what happens next? You will need your pass notification letter when applying for indefinite leave to remain (settlement) in the UK or, if you've previously been granted settlement, to apply for British Citizenship via naturalisation. You will find more information about making these applications in Chapter One: Introducing the Life in the UK Test.

Citizenship is the ultimate goal for many immigrants to the UK and it's something that the government is actively encouraging. At the time of writing (summer 2008), a major shake up of Britain's immigration system was being considered, which, if agreed by Parliament, would lead to changes for would-be residents and citizens from late 2009.

EARNED CITIZENSHIP

The reforms are designed to make the immigration system simpler for both migrants and the UK public to follow; however, they also make the journey to citizenship longer and make increased demands on those wishing to stay in the UK, either as residents or citizens. The plan is called 'earned citizenship' and it consists of three key stages:

> 1. Temporary residence

> 2. Probationary citizenship

> 3. British citizenship/permanent residence

When and if these changes become law, migrants will need to meet certain requirements in order to pass from one stage to the next. One of these will be taking and passing the Life in the UK test.

Temporary Residence

This is similar to the period of time a migrant currently spends in the UK before applying for settlement (ILR) – and the requirements are also similar. Under the new rules there are three routes to citizenship and three groups of people who could qualify:

♦ Those applying as economic migrants (designated as 'highly skilled' or 'skilled' workers) and their dependents: this group would need to remain in employment and pay taxes.

♦ People applying as family members, such as spouses and civil partners; this group would need to be able to prove their continuing relationship, and support themselves with the help of their sponsor.

♦ Those in need of protection, such as asylum seekers and their dependents: this group would be allowed to stay if they could show they faced a real risk of danger and harm in their home country.

It's expected that the periods of temporary residence would be similar to the current qualifying periods – usually between two and five years, depending on your reason for being in the UK – but at the end of the period you would need to progress on to probationary citizenship or leave the UK. One of the requirements for probationary citizenship would be passing the Life in the UK test or obtaining an ESOL with citizenship certificate.

> Evidence suggests that fluency in English increases the chance of employment in the UK for an immigrant from an ethnic minority by around 22 per cent and raises their likely earnings by up to 20 per cent.

Probationary Citizenship

This stage represents the biggest change from the current system. It would replace the stage of indefinite leave to remain or ILR. Instead, applicants would become probationary (provisional) citizens, the length of which would depend on the following:

♦ Whether or not you intend to apply for citizenship at the end of it: the new rules would encourage people to do this by allowing them to apply after a minimum of a year's probationary citizenship, while those seeking permanent residency would have to wait at least three years.

♦ Whether you become an 'active citizen': government proposals suggest that someone who does voluntary work or otherwise contributes to their community – by running a sports team, for example, or serving on a community body such as a school board – would spend a shorter time as a probationary citizen before moving on to the final stage. This could reduce probationary citizenship to one year for those seeking to become British citizens.

♦ Whether you stay within the law: even minor offenders might see the length of their probationary period increased, while those convicted of more serious offences would not be allowed to become probationary citizens and would have to leave the UK.

British Citizenship or Permanent Residence?

This is the stage at which applicants would complete their journey to citizenship/permanent residence. As a citizen, you would have the same rights as other British citizens, including full voting rights, the opportunity to apply for a British passport and eligibility for assistance from British consulates when abroad. At present, around 40 per cent of migrants who are granted indefinite leave to remain choose not to progress to citizenship, but the government

believes that by becoming citizens they would be more fully integrated (assimilated) into UK society.

Under the proposed new rules, those who cannot apply for citizenship, e.g. people from countries which don't allow dual nationality, could opt for permanent residency instead, but would have to wait longer: up to five years, or three years if they make a contribution to their community through voluntary or charity work. The shorter progression time to British citizenship from probationary citizenship is to encourage those who have a choice to opt for citizenship over permanent residence.

Only after gaining British citizenship or permanent residence would migrants have access to the full range of welfare benefits.

In 2007, a record 164,635 applications for British citizenship were approved by the UK government. The main nationalities granted British citizenship were Indian, Filipino, Afghan, South African and Pakistani.

HOW WILL THE CHANGES AFFECT YOU?

How much any changes to the immigration laws will affect you depends on what stage of the immigration process you've reached – and when you're reading this book!

Anyone who gains indefinite leave to remain before any revisions to the immigration system become law should be able progress towards citizenship – or not – as described in **Chapter One**. However, laws can change at any time, and proposed changes can be revised in line with public opinion, therefore it's vital that you check the latest information by visiting the UK Border Agency's website (www.ukba. homeoffice.gov.uk).

THE CITIZENSHIP CEREMONY

Whatever route you take to British Citizenship, it will end with a citizenship ceremony, and these take place in town halls and register offices across the country. They're organised by local authorities, and up to 24 new citizens usually receive their citizenship certificate at the same ceremony.

It's a formal occasion and you're expected to take it seriously – for example, you'll have to stand while Britain's National Anthem, *God Save the Queen*, is played. It's also an enjoyable one, as you can invite your friends and family to join your celebration, and sometimes the local mayor will also attend. There's no charge, as the cost is covered by your citizenship application fee.

You'll be invited to a citizenship ceremony, usually by your local authority, after receiving your letter from the UK Borders Agency confirming that citizenship has been granted. You must attend, and have 90 days from being granted citizenship to attend a ceremony – if you don't, you'll have to go through (and pay for) the whole application process again!

The most significant event at the citizenship ceremony is when you take the oath of allegiance to the Queen and pledge (promise) your loyalty to Britain: this is the moment that you become a British citizen.

The Oath of Allegiance

This declaration of loyalty to Britain and the Queen, which outlines your responsibilities as a British citizen, is as follows:

> *I (your name) swear by Almighty God that, on becoming a British citizen, I will be faithful and bear true allegiance to Her Majesty Queen Elizabeth the Second, Her Heirs and Successors according to law.*
>
> *I will give my loyalty to the United Kingdom and respect its rights and freedoms. I will uphold its democratic values. I will observe its laws faithfully and fulfil my duties and obligations as a British citizen.*

There's no need to memorise the oath, as you will repeat the words spoken by an official. Once you've sworn the oath, you will receive your citizenship certificate. You will need this when applying for a British passport.

YOUR RIGHTS AS A BRITISH CITIZEN

British citizens are protected by the Human Rights Act 1998 which awards them the rights of liberty, respect for their private life, freedom of speech and protection against discrimination, among others. In addition, UK law also provides you with some other specific rights, such as:

♦ **Security**: your personal data must be kept secure by the agencies which use it – this right is upheld by the Data Protection Act and stops people accessing your medical records or bank accounts.

♦ **Health and medical treatment**: you have the right to obtain free healthcare when you need it.

♦ **Education**: you and your children have the right to free education.

♦ **Access to information**: you have the right to obtain information from government and other public bodies under the Freedom of Information Act – this can include what they spend your money on, and how much.

◆ **Work**: you have the right to work without restriction, and to receive the legal minimum wage for the work you do.

◆ **Home**: you have the right to be housed by your local authority if you're classed as vulnerable.

Registering to Vote

As a British citizen you also have the right to vote in local, general and European elections, provided you're aged over 18 and not in prison or mentally ill. First, you need to register to vote, which you do by applying to have your name added to the electoral register, which is a list of people who live in each constituency (voting area) and are eligible to vote.

Each year in September and October, the local authority sends out an electoral register form to each household, in order to maintain an up-to-date list of eligible voters. However, if you don't want to wait, you can phone the council and ask them to send you a form or you can do it online (💻 www.aboutmyvote.co.uk).

It's against the law not to complete and return the electoral register form. However, once your name is on the register – unlike in some countries – there's no obligation to vote. Having your name on the electoral register is a good way for companies and organisations to confirm your address. This is useful if you need to obtain a loan or other credit, which you may find more difficult if you aren't on the electoral register.

Applying for a British Passport

A British passport is one of the most sought after documents in the world. Not only does it allow you to travel and work without restriction throughout the European Union, it also makes it much easier to travel to other countries around the world. Many countries, including the US and Australia, have a list of nationalities which either don't need a visa for a short visit or can obtain one on arrival, and UK passport holders are usually on that list. That's not to say you won't need a visa to travel to some countries, but a British passport certainly opens doors for you.

A British passport is also a reliable and useful means of identification, either in the UK or abroad. British citizens don't carry identity (ID) cards – although the government has announced it's planning to introduce them for foreign nationals from late 2008 – and the next best thing is a UK passport.

To apply for your new passport, you can obtain a form from the post office. As well as providing details of your citizenship certificate, you will need two photographs which must be countersigned by someone who has a position of importance in the community and has known you for at least two years. This might be a doctor, teacher, minister of religion or someone similar, and they must hold a British or Irish passport.

A new passport costs £72 (mid-2008) and the application form is quite complicated, although it'll be a breeze after your citizenship application form! There's the option of having it checked by someone at the post office for a small extra cost. Leave plenty of time between applying for your passport and planning a trip abroad. From 2007, the government was planning to introduce interviews for some first-time passport applicants, to safeguard against identity theft, therefore you should allow at least six weeks in case you're called for an interview.

For more information about applying for a passport, call the Home Office Identity and Passport Service's Passport Adviceline (☎ 0870-521 0410) or visit 💻 www.ips.gov.uk/passport/index.asp).

Guardsman, London

APPENDICES

APPENDIX A: USEFUL CONTACTS

The following list of organisations can provide extra background information on subjects covered in this book. There's no need to learn all about them for the Life in the UK test – any details you need have been included in chapters two to six. However, they may help you to better understand some of the chapters, and provide a useful information resource in the UK.

Education, Careers & Children

Careers Wales – ☎ 0800-100900, 🖥 www.careerswales.com.

Careers Scotland – ☎ 0845-850 2502, 🖥 www.careers-scotland.org.uk.

Childcare Link – advice on finding a registered childminder (☎ 0800-234 6346, 🖥 www.childcarelink.gov.uk, Scottish Childcare, 🖥 www.scottishchildcare.gov.uk).

Connexions – careers advice for young people in England (☎ 080-800 13219, 🖥 www.connexions-direct.com).

Department for Children, Schools and Families – government department focusing on education, children and young people (☎ 0870-000 2288, 🖥 www.dfes.gov.uk).

Employment & Work

Advisory, Conciliation and Arbitration Service (ACAS) – information about your rights at work (☎ 0845-747 4747, 🖥 www.acas.org.uk),

Business Link – advice on grants and loans available to self-employed people (☎ 0845-600 9006, 🖥 www.businesslink.gov.uk).

Commission for Equality and Human Rights – help dealing with discrimination (England ☎ 0845-604 6610, Scotland ☎ 0845-604 5510, Wales ☎ 0845-604 8810, 🖥 www.equalityhumanrights.com).

Equality Commission for Northern Ireland – deals with discrimination in Northern Ireland (☎ 028-9089 0890, 🖥 www.equalityni.org).

Home Office Criminal Records Bureau – information about CRB checks (☎ 0870-909 0811, 🖥 www.crb.gov.uk; Disclosure Scotland ☎ 0870-609 6006, 🖥 www.disclosurescotland.co.uk).

Jobcentre Plus/Jobseeker Direct – government agency advertising job vacancies and training opportunities and advising on benefits (☎ 0845-606 0234, 🖥 www.jobcentreplus.gov.uk).

Learndirect – careers advice, courses and training options (☎ 0800-100900, 🖳 www. learndirect-advice.co.uk).

Minimum Wage Helpline – check whether you're being paid enough (☎ 0845-600 0678).

National Recognition Information Centre – find out whether your qualifications are valid in the UK (☎ 0870-990 4088, 🖳 www.naric.org.uk).

Trades Union Congress (TUC) – information about trade unions and what they can do for you (🖳 www.tuc.org.uk).

Working for Yourself – advice from HM Revenue and Customs for the newly self-employed (☎ 0845-915 4515, 🖳 www.hmrc.gov.uk/pdfs/ir56.htm).

Worksmart – advice on careers and surviving the world of work from the Trades Union Congress (🖳 www.worksmart.org.uk).

Health

Family Planning Association – advice about contraception (☎ 0845-310 1334, 🖳 www.fpa. org.uk).

National Health Service – England 🖳 www.nhs.uk; Scotland 🖳 www.show.scot.nhs.uk/findnearest/healthservices; Wales 🖳 www.wales.nhs.uk/directory.cfm; Northern Ireland 🖳 www.n-i.nhs.uk.

NHS Direct – health advice over the phone (☎ 0845-4647; Scotland NHS24 ☎ 0845-424 2424).

NHS Direct Online – health advice on the internet (🖳 www.nhsdirect.nhs.uk; Scotland 🖳 www.nhs24.com).

Immigration & Citizenship

UK Border Agency (UKBA) – government information on immigration and citizenship, with downloadable application forms (Lunar House, 40 Wellesley Road, Croydon, Surrey, CR9 2BY, ☎ 0870-606 7766, 🖳 www.ukba.homeoffice.gov.uk).

◆ Citizenship enquiries: ☎ 0845-010 5200.

◆ Asylum enquiries: ☎ 0845-602 1739.

◆ Nationality Checking Service for people applying for citizenship: 🖳 www.bia.homeoffice. gov.uk/britishcitizenship/applying/checkingservice.

Life in the UK Test & ESOL (English Language) Courses

Department of Innovation, Universities and Skills (DIUS) – government department in charge of further education (☎ 020-7215 5555).

Directgov – government information on courses to learn English for Speakers of Other Languages (🖳 www.direct.gov.uk/en/EducationAndLearning/AdultLearning/ImprovingYourSkills/DG_10037499).

Learndirect – a guide to Skills for Life courses, including ESOL (☎ 0800-150450, 💻 www.learndirect.co.uk).

Life in the UK Test – official helpline and website for the test, with a full list of test centres (☎ 0800-015 4245, 💻 www.lifeintheuktest.gov.uk).

UK Online – for centres giving access to computers and the internet, so that you can practise the test (☎ 0800-771234, 💻 www.ukonlinecentres.com/consumer).

Tax, National Insurance & Pensions

HM Revenue and Customs – for information about all aspects of tax, National Insurance and tax credits (💻 www.hmrc.gov.uk).

National Insurance Registrations Helpline – how to register for an NI number (☎ 0845-915 7006)

Pensions Advisory Service – advice on occupational and private pensions (☎ 0845-601 2923, 💻 www.opas.org.uk).

Pension Service Helpline – advice on government State Pensions (☎ 0845-606 0265, 💻 www.thepensionservice.gov.uk).

Travel & Transport

Driver and Vehicle Licensing Agency (DVLA) – information about driving licences and making sure your vehicle is road legal (driver information ☎ 0870-240 0009, vehicle information ☎ 0870-240 0010, 💻 www.dvla.gov.uk).

Home Office Identity and Passport Service – information about applying for a British passport and the new identity card system (Passport Adviceline ☎ 0870-521 0410, 💻 www.ips.gov.uk).

National Express – the UK's largest coach network (☎ 0870-580 8080, 💻 www.nationalexpress.com).

National Rail Enquiry Service – advice about train travel (☎ 0845-748 4950, 💻 www.nationalrail.co.uk).

UK & Local Government

About My Vote – put your name on the electoral register (💻 www.aboutmyvote.co.uk).

Contact your Member of Parliament: House of Commons, Westminster, London SW1A 0AA (☎ 020-7729 3000).

Electoral Commission – information about elections and the electoral process (💻 www.electoralcommission.org.uk; Northern Ireland – Electoral Office for Northern Ireland, ☎ 028-9044 6688).

Local Government Association – find out the name of your local authority (☎ 020-7664 3131).

Northern Ireland Assembly – information about Northern Ireland's devolved government (💻 www.niassembly.gov.uk).

Scottish Parliament – information and visiting times (The Scottish Parliament, Edinburgh, EH99 1SP, ☎ 0131-348 5200, 💻 www. scottish.parliament.uk).

UK Parliament – what's happening at Britain's seat of government (💻 www.parliament.uk).

UK Statistics Authority – facts and figures, including census statistics (💻 www.statistics.gov.uk).

Welsh Assembly – to arrange a visit (☎ 029-2089 8477, 💻 www.new.wales.gov.uk/splash).

Write to Them – find out the details of your local councillors, MP and other representatives and write to them (💻 www.writetothem.com).

Utilities & Services

British Telecom – the main UK phone company (💻 www.bt.com).

Energywatch – find out which company supplies your electricity and telephone service and obtain advice about changing suppliers (☎ 0845-906 0708).

Office of Communications (Ofcom) – for information about different telephone and television service providers (💻 www.ofcom.org.uk).

Television Licensing – how to obtain a TV licence (☎ 0870-576 3763).

Transco – find out who supplies your gas, and report a gas leak (☎ 0870-608 1524).

Miscellaneous

BBC – the website of the British Broadcasting Corporation has news in over 40 languages, plus weather, a section on learning English and many other useful sources of information (💻 www.bbc.co.uk).

Citizens Advice Bureau – the CAB is an independent organisation with trained advisors who help with problems across a wide range of topics, including health, housing, immigration issues, consumer problems, money and debt, employment and work problems. It can also provide legal help and interpreters (💻 www.nacab.org.uk, or see the CAB information site, 💻 www.adviceguide.org.uk).

Directgov – public service information on everything from employment and tax to health and transport (💻 www.direct.gov.uk).

Fire and Rescue Services – for information about fire safety and details of your local fire service (💻 www.fire.gov.uk).

Yellow Pages – a directory of local services, which is supplied free to each home in the UK (💻 www.yell.com).

APPENDIX B: BRITISH CULTURE

This chapter includes some useful facts, and fun information about British culture. The content isn't a part of the Life in the UK test, so you don't have to learn it, but it will help you to understand more about your new homeland. See also our sister publication, *Culture Wise England.*

Television

Some popular TV programmes which are typically British are listed below:

Soaps

Coronation Street – one of the longest-running soaps, 'Corrie' is set on a street in northern England, where everyone gathers at the Rovers Return pub.

EastEnders – set in London's Albert Square, and populated by a mixed bunch of Cockneys who gather in the Queen Vic pub.

Emmerdale – life in a village in the Yorkshire Dales; the meeting place is (you guessed!) a pub, called the Woolpack.

Comedy

Blackadder – an upper-class bully whose adventures take place during different times in British history.

Dad's Army – a group of middle-aged men 'defend' their corner of England during the Second World War.

Fawlty Towers – set in the worst hotel in Britain, run by the bizarre Basil Fawlty, this is considered by many to be the best UK sitcom series of all time.

Have I Got News for You – a panel game which reinvents the news while mocking public figures.

Keeping Up Appearances – snobby Hyacinth Bucket rules her husband in a suburban comedy of manners.

The Kumars at No 42 – comedy with an untypical Asian family.

Little Britain and **The Fast Show** – comic sketches built around modern British stereotypes.

Monty Python – if you can understand this classic comedy show, you're halfway to understanding the British sense of humour.

The Office – a funny picture of life in a British workplace.

Only Fools and Horses – survival and cunning on a South London council estate.

Till Death Us Do Part – controversial comedy from the '60s and '70s which features a racist old man as its central character.

Drama

Auf Wiedersehen, Pet – British builders go to work in Germany.

The Bill – long-running drama set in a London police station.

Boys from the Blackstuff – set in the '80s and following the lives of five men who struggle with unemployment in a Britain run by Margaret Thatcher.

Casualty and ***Holby City*** – life and love in the National Health Service.

Any costume drama – from *Brideshead Revisited* to *Pride and Prejudice*, British television excels at turning its history into drama.

Anything by Dennis Potter – TV writer whose dramas, such as *The Singing Detective* and *Pennies from Heaven*, paint a dark but fascinating picture of British life.

Doctor Who – cult classic featuring an eccentric time traveller who's been wandering the universe since the '60s.

House of Cards – corruption and power struggles in the Houses of Parliament.

Inspector Morse – one of TV's best-loved detectives solves crime and crosswords in the university town of Oxford.

Midsomer Murders – whodunit set in a pretty English village where murders take place every week!

Talking Heads – a series of monologues (dramas featuring one person) written by Alan Bennett which feature some of the best-written British characters ever seen on TV.

Upstairs, Downstairs – historical drama showing the lives of masters and servants in a London townhouse during the first three decades of the 20th century.

Films

Alfie – the life and loves of a Cockney womaniser in the '60s – see the original Michael Caine version.

Billy Elliot – coalminer's son from County Durham wants to be a ballet dancer.

Brief Encounter – this '40s romance in a train station waiting room is a perfect example of British good manners and the stiff upper lip.

Braveheart – the story of William Wallace and his fight for an independent Scotland in the 13th century.

Any *Carry On* film – low-budget British comedy which illustrates the UK's love of sexual innuendo and slapstick.

Dirty Pretty Things – thriller set among London's community of illegal immigrants, with a clever twist at the end.

Four Weddings and a Funeral – comedy drama written around two of the most important rites of passage in British life.

Get Carter – violent crime drama among '70s Britain's underworld.

The Full Monty – six jobless steelworkers in Sheffield become male strippers.

Kes – Yorkshire boy befriends a kestrel as he tries to escape his future as a miner.

Hope and Glory – family drama set in Second World War London at the time of the Blitz bombings.

The Lavender Hill Mob – classic comedy from the '50s about a bunch of unlikely thieves in south London.

Life is Sweet – a lower-working class family in London struggle for survival.

Love Actually – romantic comedy in which the Prime Minister, and a host of other characters, find love as Britain gets ready for Christmas.

My Beautiful Launderette – love, homosexuality and racism in '80s Britain.

The Queen – award-winning drama goes behind the scenes at Buckingham Palace after the death of Princess Diana.

Trainspotting – acclaimed drama about a group of heroin addicts surviving in Edinburgh in the '90s.

This Is England – racism and growing pains, as a boy on a council estate in Nottingham joins a group of skinheads (an '80s cult) during the time of the Falklands War.

The *Wallace and Gromit* films– award-winning animations about a man and his dog in Yorkshire, who have a love of weird inventions and Wensleydale cheese.

Withnail and I – two unemployed actors escape from North London to the countryside, for a holiday which doesn't quite go to plan.

Books

I f you can cope with reading classic novels, anything by Charles Dickens, Emily Brontë or Jane Austen is a good place to start, for a look at British culture in the 18th and 19th centuries. You can also try dipping into William Shakespeare's plays, which are a cornerstone of British literature, or the Sherlock Holmes detective novels by Sir Arthur Conan Doyle. More recent authors and books which are essentially British include:

Pat Barker – her Regeneration trilogy is a challenging read, but also a stunning portrayal of survival during and after the First World War.

Enid Blyton – the classic British children's author.

Bill Bryson – his travel book *Notes from a Small Island* neatly sums up the British character.

Frances Hodgson Burnett – *The Secret Garden* is a children's classic set in upper-class 19th century Britain.

Culture Wise England – cultural know-how from Survival Books.

Helen Fielding – the life and loves of an ordinary modern British girl in *Bridget Jones's Diary*.

Kate Fox – excellent examination of English culture in *Watching the English: The Hidden Rules of English Behaviour*.

Kenneth Grahame – children's fiction about a group of animals who live on a riverbank in *The Wind in the Willows.*

Mark Haddon – An autistic boy investigates the death of his neighbour's dog and discovers the truth about himself in *The Curious Incident of the Dog in the Night-Time.*

Michelle Magorian – *Goodnight Mister Tom* tells the story of a grumpy old man who looks after a boy evacuated from London during the Second World War.

George Mikes – A Hungarian's view of the British in *How to be a Brit.*

C S Lewis – The *Chronicles of Narnia* are fantasy stories for children set against a background of middle-class England in the '30s and '40s.

Jeremy Paxman – presents a fascinating portrait of English people in his book *The English.*

JK Rowling – the adventures of the boy wizard Harry Potter – a series of seven all-time best-sellers that are credited with getting millions of children reading.

Zadie Smith – *White Teeth* tells the tale of the friendship between an Englishman and a Bangladeshi living in London in the late 20th century.

WC Sellar and RJ Yeatman – *1066 and All That: A Memorable History Of England* is a tongue-in-cheek reworking of British history.

Sue Townsend – a look at '80s Britain through the eyes of a teenage boy in the *Adrian Mole* books, while *The Queen and I* is an amusing observation of what happens when Britain's Monarch is deposed and sent to live in a council house.

Keith Waterhouse – *Billy Liar* is a working-class Yorkshire boy who lives in a fantasy world.

The Xenophobe's Guide to the English – a fun and honest look at the English way of life.

Music

For typically British classical music, try *Land of Hope and Glory*, **Edward Elgar's patriotic song, which many people think would be a better national anthem than** *God Save the Queen*. **Scotland, Wales and Northern Ireland have their share of folk and cultural music, too. Some of the rock and pop artists who best represent Britain include:**

The Beatles	Led Zeppelin	Specials
Black Sabbath	New Order	Spice Girls
Blur	Madness	The Rolling Stones
The Clash	Oasis	
Elvis Costello	Pink Floyd	Van Morrison
Deep Purple	Queen	The Who
Genesis	Sex Pistols	
The Jam	The Smiths	

The Royal Family

In addition to Queen Elizabeth the second and her eldest son, Prince Charles the Prince of Wales, there are many more members of Britain's first family. The best-known are:

Prince Philip – The Queen's husband (or consort), who is also known as The Duke of Edinburgh.

Prince William – The eldest son of Prince Charles and his first wife, Diana, Princess of Wales, William is second in line to become King after Prince Charles.

Prince Harry – The younger son of Charles and Diana.

Prince Andrew – The Duke of York is the third child of the Queen and Prince Philip.

Princess Anne – The Queen's only daughter, Princess Anne is the only member of the royal family to have competed in the Olympic Games (and won a gold medal in equestrian).

Prince Edward – The Earl of Wessex is the youngest child of Queen Elizabeth II and Prince Philip.

Regional Specialities

Here are a few of the landmarks, foods, symbols and other icons which distinguish different parts of the UK. If you don't know who or what they are, check them on the internet!

Cornwall – Cornish pasties, Land's End, Rick Stein, Eden Project, surfing, tin mining

Cumbria – Beatrix Potter, Kendal mint cake, Lake District, Scafell Pike, William Wordsworth

East Anglia – beach huts, Colman's mustard, Delia Smith, Norfolk Broads

Liverpool – The Beatles, the Liver Building, Red Rum, Scouse (a dialect and a meat stew), the Kop, Superlambanana

London – Barbara Windsor, Bond Street, jellied eels, London Eye, Routemaster buses, Thames

Manchester – *Coronation Street*, fish and chips, Manchester United, Rusholme's Curry Mile

Midlands – balti curries, Birmingham's Rotunda, canals, Lenny Henry, Nottingham's Goose Fair, Staffordshire bull terrier

Newcastle –Angel of the North, Newcastle Brown Ale, Gazza, Tyne Bridge

Northern Ireland – flax, George Best, Giants Causeway, hurling, soda bread, Ulster fry

Scotland – bagpipes, Ben Nevis, Billy Connolly, haggis, Stone of Scone, tartan, scotch whisky

South East – Brighton beach, Channel Tunnel, hops, Essex girls, Royal Ascot, White Cliffs of Dover

Wales – Catherine Zeta Jones, daffodils, leeks, mining, Rugby football, sheep, Snowdon, Tom Jones

The West Country – cider, Cheddar Gorge, Glastonbury Festival, Stonehenge, Thomas Hardy, Bath

Yorkshire – Betty's Tea Rooms, Fred Trueman, moors, Wensleydale cheese, whippets, York Minster, white rose, Yorkshire pudding

APPENDIX C: GLOSSARY

A

Absent from work: not at work, e.g. because of illness or injury.

Abusive: violent or unkind behaviour, generally towards another person.

Academic course: a series of lessons in which students learn by studying information from books or other media. (also see **Vocational Course**)

Access (internet): a connection.

Accountant: a person who keeps business records to work out the money made or lost by a person or business, and who will advise on tax, national insurance and other matters.

AD: Anno Domini, used as a time reference dating from the birth of Christ (also see **BC**).

Addictive substance: usually a type of drug or chemical substance to which a person appears to need regular access, its use often being almost impossible to stop without specialist medical assistance.

Adultery: sex between a married person and someone who is not his or her wife or husband.

Afford: to have the funds needed to be able to pay for something.

Allegiance: loyalty or faithfulness to, say, a country or a leader.

Amphetamine: an addictive, illegal and powerful drug (see **Addictive substance**).

Annexation: the (usually) forceful takeover of a neighbouring country.

Anonymous information: information given by an unknown person.

Ante-natal care: the medical care given to a pregnant woman and her unborn baby.

Applicant (employment): someone who requests a job from an employer, often by letter or by filling in an application form.

Application letter: a formal letter sent to an employer, requesting (applying for) a job.

Appoint (employment): to formally offer to job to a suitable applicant.

Arbitrary (law): not bound by law or by rules, and often considered to be unfair.

Aristocracy: traditionally, very wealthy people born into the highest class in society, and referred to as **aristocrats**.

Armed forces: the navy, army and air force which defend a country in times of both peace and war.

Arrested (police): being removed to a police station, and being kept there for a certain amount of time in order to answer questions about unlawful actions or activity (see **Detained by the Police**).

Assault: the criminal act of using physical force upon another – for example, punching or kicking a person.

Assessment methods (education): ways of measuring students' abilities or skills, using a variety of practical or mental tests.

Asylum: a place of safety for people who are accused of crime in another country.

Asylum seekers: people who formally apply to stay in another country because their own is no longer a place of safely for them, perhaps for political reasons (see **Refugees**).

B

Ban: something officially forbidden, or to officially forbid.

Bank Holiday: a public holiday for banks and businesses, and an official day off for most working people.

Baron: a man who belongs to the lower ranks of British nobility.

BC: used as a time reference to the number of years before the birth of Christ (also see **AD**).

Betting shop: a place to gamble money on the results of horse-racing, football matches or similar.

Bid (money): to make an offer for something which has not been allocated a fixed price, with the highest bidder being sold the item.

Binding, legally: this describes an agreement which, by law, cannot be changed. Withdrawal is also not an option.

Birth certificate: an official document which states the name, birth-place and birth-date of an individual, and the names and occupations of his/her parents.

Birth parent: a person who is the natural, biological parent of a child.

Birth rate: the number of babies born in a particular year or place, expressed as a percentage of a population.

Bishop: a senior Christian priest who heads the different churches in a designated area.

Boom: a sharp rise in business activity, for example.

Bound, legally: acting in a way that is lawful.

Breach of contract: the breaking of a legal agreement.

British Empire: states under British colonial rule, at one time accounting for one quarter of the world's population. Many are now independent, the rest being collectively known as the Commonwealth of Nations.

Broker (finance): a person who advises and selects the most suitable and economic services in fields such as insurance and mortgages, and sometimes called a financial adviser.

Brutality: cruel, harmful and violent behaviour towards another person.

Building Society: an institution similar to a bank, and which can be used for savings or house loans (see also **Mortgage**).

Built-up area: areas with many buildings and few open spaces, and where many people live and work.

Bureaux de Change: places for exchanging one currency for another.

Burglary: the criminal act of stealing from a building (also see **Theft**).

Bursary: a grant given to a student, by a university, to enable further study.

Business accounts: official business records from which profit and loss is calculated before the payment of tax due to the government (see also **Accountant**).

By-election: an election caused by the death or resignation of an MP, to replace him or her in Parliament before the next general election.

C

Cabinet (government): senior ministers responsible for controlling government policy.

Cable Company: a supplier of telephone or cable television connections.

Cannabis: an illegal drug, usually smoked.

Captivity: a state of imprisonment, with no free movement.

Carriageway: a single carriageway has only one lane of traffic; another lane takes traffic in the opposite direction.

A dual carriageway: a road wide enough for two lanes of traffic, divided from another road taking traffic in the opposite direction.

Cast a vote (government): to formally choose from several options which will enable a group parliamentary decision to be made.

Casualties (medical): people wounded through, for example, an accident or war.

Caution (employment law): a formal warning.

Cautious: careful, not wanting to take risks.

Census (government): an official count of the population, possibly containing details of some of their personal information.

Charity, give to: donate money, or otherwise act to help people suffering from illness, poverty or starvation, for example.

Charter (government): an official written statement describing the rights and responsibilities of a country and its people.

Chieftain: a Scottish clan leader.

Childminder: a person, usually trained and qualified, who is entrusted with the care of young children during their parents' absence.

Circulate (money): to pass from one person to another on a continual basis.

Civil disobedience: unlawful behaviour by members of the public, often for political reasons.

Civil law: the legal system for dealing with disputes between people or groups.

Civil service: government departments which manage running the country – people who work in this capacity are called civil servants.

Clamp (transport, police): a metal device placed on the wheel of a car in order to immobilise it (often because of illegal parking) – the driver has then to pay to have the clamp removed.

Clan: families or groups of people who live under the authority of a chieftain, and who are sometimes descendants of a common ancestor – this is a term traditionally used in Scotland.

Clarification (language): a clear way of stating something in a way that can be easily understood.

Clergy: officials of the Christian church, e.g. bishops and priests.

Coalition: an alliance between political parties who decide that they can work together.

Cocaine: an illegal drug which is both addictive and powerful, and which is occasionally prescribed by doctors to relieve pain (see **Addictive substance**).

Code of practice: set rules and procedures which workers are expected to honour and to work within.

Colleagues: co-workers in the same company – often with professional jobs.

Colonise: to take over another country and live in it, for the benefit and greater wealth of the home country.

Commemorate: to perform an act of remembrance, usually on a particular day.

Commit a crime: to do something which is unlawful.

Commonwealth of Nations: an association of Britain, those states still ruled by it and its former colonised states – the British monarchy is accepted by the associated states as their ruler.

Community events: local area organised events which benefit those living in the same locality: for example, a fund-raising event to buy particular equipment for a local hospital.

Compensation (money): money paid to one who has suffered injury or loss in some way: compensation can be paid if a person has been treated unfairly or illegally by his or her employer.

Compulsory testing: tests required to be done by law.

Concern: anxiety about an important thing or problem.

Concession: a right given to end a disagreement or stalemate.

Condemn to death: a decision by a judge to mete out the most severe punishment possible, because of a particularly serious crime – (the death penalty is no longer allowed in the UK).

Confidential information: private information known only to the giver and receiver of it.

Confiscate (law): to legally remove possessions or property from the owner of them.

Conquered: having been overcome in battle.

Consecutive: following one another without interruption; e.g. meetings following on two consecutive days, over a Monday and Tuesday.

Constituency: a specific region where voters (constituents) who live there can elect an MP to be their Parliamentary representative.

Constitution (law): established laws and principles, legally structured to govern a country.

Consumer problems: problems that are to do with things that people bought or services they paid for.

Contraception: birth-control methods to prevent sexually-active women from becoming pregnant, e.g. 'the pill' and IUDs.

Contributions (finance): regular payments towards something of worth, e.g. a pension.

Convention (government): an agreement made between countries, concerning rules and behaviour.

Corrupt (behaviour): illegal and dishonest acts.

Coverage (media): press reports that can be read in the newspapers (see

Free Press).

Credit card: a card used to buy goods or services which are paid for by a credit company – the company is then paid by the card-holder, following a monthly bill (see **Debit Card**).

Criminal: a person found guilty of breaking the law.

Criminal offence: an illegal activity for which a person may face prosecution.

Crusades: wars fought to try to promote Christianity.

Currency (money): the system of money used by a country or group of countries.

Cut off (service): to disconnect a supply.

D

Debate: a discussion – or to discuss and give different opinions about something.

Debit Card: a card used to buy goods or services, with payment automatically coming from money in a bank or building society account (see **Credit Card**).

Decline in number: to fall or reduce in number.

Decree (law): an official decision or order.

Defeat: to beat someone by strength or by sharper skills.

Defer: to delay until later.

Degrading (treatment): treatment that causes great distress and humiliation (**see Humiliated**).

Democratic country: a country where those who govern are elected by its people to represent them in Parliament.

Deport: to force an illegal immigrant, for example, to return to his or her own country.

Deposit (housing): a sum of money paid to the landlord of a rented property – when the person leaves, if the property and furnishings have not been in any way damaged, the deposit is returned.

Deposit (money): a sum of money taken as a down-payment – the balance must be paid later.

Descent, of: coming originally from – e.g. 'being of British descent' describes being a British family member (see **Roots, Ethnic Origin**).

Desert someone (law): to leave someone without care or help, e.g. to leave a wife or husband.

Detained by the police: being kept at a police station whilst awaiting further questioning (see **Arrested**).

Detect crimes (police): to discover information about illegal actions or activities.

Devolution: the passing of power from a central government to a regional or local group – this can then be described as a devolved administration.

Dialect: a form of language spoken by particular people from a certain social group or local area.

Direct debit: a regular transfer of money from one account to another which is activated by the recipient.

Disability, physical/mental: a condition which makes it difficult for a person to do ordinary, everyday activities.

Discrimination: the act of unfair treatment to a person or persons, e.g. because of their sex, nationality, age or disability.

Dismissal (employment): removal from a job of work – sometimes called 'the sack'.

Disputes: serious disagreements about which people may take legal advice or action.

Disturbance (law): a situation where loud behaviour and acts of violence upset and distress members of the public.

Divorce: the legal act of ending a marriage.

Domestic policies: political decisions that are relative to one country only.

Domestic rates: a tax paid by residents of Northern Ireland towards the provision of local services by their local authorities.

Domestic violence: aggressive acts in the home which cause mental or physical harm to family members.

Dominion: a self-governing country which was once colonised.

Dump: to throw something away – often leaving it in an unsuitable place.

Dwelling: a place to live.

Dynasty: a situation where power and authority is passed down through family members over a long period.

E

Ecstasy: a dangerous and illegal drug, which causes its users to feel full of energy, but which can cause death (see **Addictive substance**).

Elect a person: to choose a person by vote.

Electoral register: the official list of those allowed a vote in an election.

Electorate: all who are permitted to vote in an election.

Eligible: allowed by law.

Emergency services: services that may be alerted by telephone, and which will offer urgent assistance, e.g. the police, ambulance or fire services, or the coastguard and lifeguard services.

Employ: to give someone paid work to do.

Employee: one who is given paid work by an employer.

Employer: a company or person that gives paid work to others.

Engagement (family): an agreement between two people that they will marry at some future date (see **Fiancé** and **Fiancée**).

Enterprise: the business energy to start and run a business.

Entitled (law): legally allowed (to do something).

Entrepreneurial: prepared to take risks, financially, to start or further promote business activities.

Ethnic minority: people who are of a different race from the majority in a particular country.

Ethnic origin: the place from which a person's family came – their country of birth, their race or nationality, perhaps including their customs (see **Roots**).

European Union (or EU): a political and economical group of European countries which encourage trade and cooperation between themselves.

Evict (housing): to legally remove someone from the place in which they live.

Evidence, collecting: seeking and obtaining information that shows without any doubt that something has actually occurred (see **Proof**).

Exchange rate: the exchange rate is the amount of money in one currency needed to buy a certain amount of money in another currency, and can vary every day (see **Bureaux de Change**).

Executed: punished by death.

Exiled: sent away to live elsewhere as an act of political punishment, with no apparent likelihood of return.

Expel: to forcefully evict someone from an organisation or country.

Exploitation: an unfair situation where someone takes advantage of others, e.g. paying them less than the minimum wage, or forcing them to work overtime.

Expression, freedom of: the liberty to discuss personal beliefs or ideas without fear of punishment from the authorities.

F

Facilities in the community: local public services such as hospitals, schools and libraries.

False statement (police): a report that contains untruthful information.

Famine: a situation in which food is in very short supply for a long time.

Fiancé: a man who has publicly stated that he's to marry a particular woman.

Fiancée: a woman who has publicly stated that she's to marry a particular man (see **Engagement**).

Fine (law): a fee that a person must pay when they have broken the law (see **On-the-spot fines**, **Penalty**).

Firearm: a gun of any kind.

First past the post: an election system in which the candidate with the highest number of votes in a particular constituency wins a parliamentary seat.

Flooding (housing): water entering a property (and also possibly causing damage to it).

Forced labour: work, usually physical, which people are made to do against their wishes.

Free Press: newspapers and other reporting media who can write freely, without any restriction from the government.

G

Gambling (money): risking money to try to win more money, e.g. in horse-racing, card-games or betting on a football match result.

Gap year (education): a year between leaving school and going on to university, during which students may travel or work abroad to gain life experience.

General election: a specific time for voters to choose their governmental representatives – in Britain, this is usually every five years.

Government policies: official beliefs and ideas embraced by a political party concerning the way that a country is governed (see **Party politics**).

Grant (money): a specific sum of money paid by an authority to help and individual or organisation to pay for something in particular, e.g. an education course or a business expansion.

Guerilla war: a small-scale war between groups of people fighting against an opposition.

Guidance (law): general advice about how or where to obtain assistance.

Guilty (law): having been found to have apparently committed a crime (see **Innocent**).

H

Hard drugs: addictive, illegal and powerful drugs.

Harassment (behaviour): offensive and bullying behaviour, occasionally found in a place of work.

Health Authority, local: an organisation which manages local health care, and which can advise on where medical help may be found.

Health hazards: risks that could harm health, e.g. smoking or excessive drinking or the use of illegal drugs.

Hearing (in court): a meeting held in court, when a judge hears evidence concerning a crime that has been committed.

Heir: someone who will legally inherit another person's possessions or position when that person dies.

Helmet: a hard hat that protects the head against injury, e.g. used by motor-cyclists or horse riders.

Heroin: an addictive, illegal and powerful drug (see **Addictive substance**).

Higher Education: a college or university education for students.

Holding public office: working for the government in service or industry.

Holy Land: a Middle East area in and around Jerusalem, where certain biblical events took place.

House of Commons: the part of the Houses of Parliament where elected MPs debate political issues.

House of Lords: the part of the Houses of Parliament where both hereditary and life-peers debate political issues.

Houses of Parliament: the seat of the British Parliament, where MPs and Lords meet, debate and pass laws.

Household: the home and its inhabitants.

Humiliated: to personally feel ashamed or embarrassed, usually in front of other people.

I

Immigration: the process of entering another country to live and work (see **Migrate**).

Inappropriate touching: touching a part of a person's body in an offensive or unacceptable way for a given situation.

Indecent remarks: words which are rude and offensive, and sometimes inappropriately sexual.

Independents (politics): MPs who represent their own ideas and beliefs rather than those of any of the main political parties.

Inflation (money): the rate at which prices rise, when set against earned income, over a period of time.

Infrastructure: a structured network necessary to operate a business or a transport system, e.g. railways or roads.

Inheritance: possessions legally inherited after the death of (usually) a relative, e.g. a daughter might inherit her father's fortune.

Inhuman (behaviour): cruel, degrading and harsh.

Innocent (law): found by a court **not** to have apparently committed a crime (see **Guilty**).

Inpatient: someone who has been found to require medical treatment for which hospitalisation is needed.

Instalments (money): regular payments (of equal amount) paid over a period of time until the total cost of something is paid, e.g. a computer that costs £500 can be paid for in ten monthly instalments of £50.

Insulting words: rude words which make people feel distressed, unhappy or ridiculed.

Insure: pay money to an insurance company, who will help to pay for repairs to damaged items, e.g. a car or a property.

Intentionally: deliberately or on purpose.

Interest (money): a percentage of money payable to a lender for the duration of a loan – or a percentage of money earned on an investment.

Internet café: a place where people can use computers to access the internet or send emails – the costs vary, according to the time the user needs.

Interpreter: a person who changes words from one language to another, without altering the meaning.

Irretrievably broken down: a particular situation which cannot be made any better by negotiation.

Islamic mortgage: an interest-free loan (see **Interest**).

J

Judge (law): the highest court official, who sees that court proceedings are lawful and fair and who decides on the punishment for a guilty criminal.

Judiciary: all judges who together are responsible for administering the law of a country in the correct way.

Jury: a group of twelve people who decide, upon listening to information, whether a person is guilty or innocent in a court of law.

L

Labour (employment): work, often physical – or a body of workers.

Landlord, landlady (housing): someone who owns a property and rents it to tenants who must pay them to live there.

Landlord, landlady (public house): the owner or manager of a public house.

Lane (transport): a narrow road, usually marked by white lines (see **Carriageway**).

Legal: allowed by law or enforced by law.

Legal Aid: money paid to a solicitor, or for court costs, which can be requested by a needy person.

Legal procedure: a lawful way.

Legislative power: the power to make laws.

Legitimate children: children of married parents.

Leisure centre: a building or area where people can pay to take part in sports and other activities for recreation purposes.

Letting agent: an organisation for the mutual service of landlords and tenants (see **Landlord, Landlady**).

Liberty: freedom.

Lock: to close something securely.

Long-standing: having existed over a long period of time.

L-plates: a sign on a car to indicate a learner-driver, and being a red 'L' in a white square.

M

Magistrate: a person who judges a court case which does not involve a serious crime.

Mainland: a piece of land which does not include any of its surrounding islands.

Manufacturer: a product-maker.

Marital status: the description of persons being single, married, separated or divorced.

Maternity leave: leave allowed to a pregnant woman or a new mother, during which time she's usually paid (see **Paternity leave**).

Maternity services: help given to mothers from early pregnancy until after their babies have been born.

Media: all public information organisations, e.g. newspapers, magazines, television, radio and the internet.

Mediation: advice and support given by a person or an organisation in order to bring an end to arguments between two persons or groups who are in disagreement.

Medical consultation: a discussion with a doctor to obtain advice and information, e.g. about illness or other health issues.

Mental illness: an illness in which a person seems to behave or think in an unusual or abnormal way, e.g. 'depression' is a mental illness which makes people unhappy and unsettled, and which can prevent them from doing ordinary routine activities.

Meter (housing): a machine that measures how much electricity, gas or water has been used in a household.

Meter reading (housing): the meter measurement which shows how much electricity, gas or water has been used.

Migrate (people): move to another country to live and work (see **Immigration**).

Military service, compulsory: the joining of the military services for a particular period of time – not compulsory in the UK.

Minor offences: illegal acts that are not considered to be serious, e.g. the theft of a small amount of money (see **Serious offences**).

Mislead (law): to give false information in order to deceive.

Missionaries: people who travel abroad to teach and spread a religious faith.

Misuse: to use wrongly.

Molestation: a sexual attack, often involving a child.

Monarch: the king or queen who reigns over a country.

Monopoly (business): a source of power having exclusive control over goods or services, and where would-be competitors are not able to deal in the same business.

Mortgage: a loan used to help to purchase a property – usually paid back in regular instalments over a period of years (see **Building Society**).

Motor (transport): a machine that causes something to move, e.g. a car.

MP: a Member of Parliament, who is elected by constituents to be their government representative.

N

National issues: political concerns that may affect all who live in a particular country.

Nationalised: bought and controlled by central government: concerns an industry or service that was originally owned privately (see **Privatise**).

Naturalised citizen: a person who is born in one country but becomes a citizen of another.

Nobility: those who belong to the highest social class in a country, some of whom may have titles, e.g. Lord or Lady (see **Aristocracy**).

Not-for-profit: a business practice in which a company or organisation does not intend to make any extra money from providing goods or services.

Notice, to give: to give advance information of a change in a future situation.

Notice (employment): a period of time to be worked after telling an employer of one's intention to leave work: or a length of time that an employer must keep someone in work, after having told them to leave.

Nuisance (behaviour): an annoyance or problem for other people to have to put up with.

O

Obstructive (behaviour): being difficult, and preventing something from happening, on purpose.

Occupy a country: to invade a country by force and to then take control of it.

Occupation (employment): a job of work.

Offensive (behaviour): upsetting or abusive.

Office, to be in: to take charge in government.

Off-licence: a store which sells alcohol in bottles or cans to be taken away and consumed elsewhere.

Olympic team: a group of sportsmen and women who represent their country in the Olympic Games, an international athletics and sporting competition held every four years.

Online: on the internet.

On-the-spot-fines: an immediate demand for money as punishment for a wrongdoing, e.g. a fine for a driving offence.

Opposition: the second-largest political party, which is not in government office.

Outpatient: a person who needs medical care in a hospital, but who can be treated without the need of an overnight stay.

P

Packaging: material that covers and protects perishable goods.

Padlock: a metal lock which can be placed on an item to secure it and to prevent anyone from stealing or opening it.

Party Politics: the commonly shared beliefs of organised political groups, e.g. the Conservative Party.

Paternity leave: a period of leave from work for a new father, during which time he will normally continue to be paid (see **Maternity leave**).

Patient (medical): someone who needs medical care from a doctor or hospital because of illness or injury.

Patriarchy: a system of society in which men and their male offspring hold power over others.

Patriotism: the pride of belonging to a particular country.

Patron Saint: a Christian Saint who is believed to protect particular people or places.

Peers: those who are members of the House of Lords in Parliament.

Penalty (law): a punishment for law-breaking.

Pension Plan, pay into a: to save money regularly towards the time when a person stops working (see **State Pension**).

Performing (theatre): publicly acting, dancing or otherwise putting on a performance of some kind.

Perishable food: food which decays and becomes inedible quickly, e.g. milk and fresh meat and fish.

Permit (law): a legal document, e.g. a work permit.

Persecuted: hunted and punished, e.g. for holding a particular religious belief.

Personal details: information used for identifying someone, e.g. their name and marital status, date of birth, home address, etc.

Personnel officer: a person whose job, within a company, is to employ staff and oversee their welfare afterwards.

Phonecard, pre-paid: a bought card that can be used to make phone calls up to the value of the card.

PIN number: four numbers which a person has to use for identification purposes when withdrawing money from their account, or when paying for something on a credit or debit card. PIN numbers should always be memorised and not divulged to anyone else.

Places of worship: churches, mosques or other religious buildings where people can pray or sing or listen to their church leaders.

Plague (medical): a disease which spreads amongst people rapidly, and from which many people die at a particular point in history.

Pluralistic society: a populace which is multi-racial and multi-cultural and which has many different ideals and beliefs.

Pocket money: a small sum of money given regularly to children so that they can buy their own sweets and toys, etc.

Pogroms: the organised massacres of many people, usually because of their race or religious views.

Pooled savings: saved money from many sources that is added together to form a larger sum of jointly-owned money.

Pope, the: the leader of the Roman Catholic Church.

Possessions: things that are owned by people, e.g. books, cars, clothes, homes.

Practise a religion: to actively live the customs of a particular religion, e.g. attend church, take part in religious services, perhaps wear special clothing.

Pregnancy: the nine-month period before the birth of a child, whilst it is growing inside its mother – the mother is then said to be pregnant.

Prehistoric: a time before the writing down of any historical records.

Prescription (medical): an official note from a doctor stating which medicine a patient needs.

Pressure group: a group of people who ask the government to try to persuade the general public to change their minds about something.

Prime Minister: the Member of Parliament who leads the political party holding power and also the whole government.

Privatised: bought and controlled by the private sector: concerns an industry or service that was originally owned by central government (see **Nationalised**).

Process of precedent: a process whereby previous decisions determine future actions (often in legal judgements).

Prohibit: to forbid or to make illegal.

Promotion (employment): a step-up to a better job within the same company.

Proof: information that shows that something has definitely happened (see **Evidence**).

Proportional representation: an electoral system where political parties may have a number of seats in Parliament that gives a true representation of their full share of all the votes cast.

Prosperity: a time of wealth or growth regarding fortune.

Provinces: area divisions within a country, for governmental reasons.

Pub: a public house – where adults of 18 and over can buy and drink alcohol.

Public, a member of: an ordinary member of the community – e.g. not a government official.

Public body: a group of people who represent the government and work for the common good of all.

Public order (law): an arrangement for rules to be obeyed in a public place.

Public place: a place which is open to all, e.g. a restaurant, cinema, park or library.

Punctual: arriving at the correct time, without being late: e.g. for work or for a doctor's appointment.

R

Racial: relating to race (see **Discrimination**).

Racially-motivated crime: a crime committed concerning racial or ethnic issues.

Racism: unpleasant behaviour towards people of another race by those who wish to be aggressive and unfair towards them.

Raising (family): caring for growing children so that they are safe and healthy.

Rape: the criminal act of enforced sex, often with violence.

Receipt (money): a piece of paper stating that something has been paid for, and given to the customer or purchaser as a record.

Recruit (employment): to find people and match them with companies or businesses who are seeking employees.

Recycle rubbish: to divide rubbish into separate materials so that each can be processed accordingly and used again.

Redundant (employment): no longer required to do a particular job – the employee may then be able to receive an amount of money as redundancy pay.

Referendum: a vote by the population or by the government to decide upon a course of action or make a political decision.

Reformation, the: a 16th century religious movement that challenged the Pope's authority, and formed Protestant churches in Europe.

Refuge: a place that is safe from danger.

Refugees: people who are forced to leave their country, sometimes for war or political reasons (see **Asylum seekers**).

Refund (money): return a sum of money to someone who has paid for something that is either unwanted or is faulty.

Remain silent (police): say nothing, and refuse to answer questions.

Rent (housing): payment to live in a room or dwelling that is owned by someone else.

Report a crime: tell the police or other authorities about an illegal action or activity.

Residence: the place where a person lives – their address.

Residential trips (school): visits to places where students will have to sleep away from home.

Resign (employment): to decide to officially terminate one's employment.

Restrict (immigration): to control the number of immigrants who wish to take up residence in a country.

Retail work: jobs that involve selling goods to customers in shops.

Retire (employment): to cease employment, often at the age of 65 or older.

Rise (in number, price): to increase, to become more expensive.

Rival viewpoints: opinions held by those in opposition to one another.

Roots (family): describes the place of someone's birth or established home.

S

Scratch card: a bought card which is rubbed with a coin to see if the buyer has won money (see **Gambling**).

Scrutinise: to examine the details closely.

Seat (government): an official position that is held by an elected Member of Parliament.

Second-hand goods: things that have already been owned by others.

Security: protection from danger.

Self-employed person: someone who works for himself/herself, and not for an employer.

Sentence (law): a period of time which must be spent in prison as punishment for a committed crime. A judge decides the length of the prison term at the end of a court case.

Separation (family): where a married couple are not divorced but live separately.

Serious misconduct (employment): unprofessional or dishonest behaviour by an employee, which may cost them their job.

Serious offences (law): wrongdoings of a serious kind, which may result in the perpetrator being sent to prison for a long time (see **Minor offences**).

Shadow Cabinet: consists of senior MPs, with special responsibilities, who belong to the governmental Opposition Party.

Sheriff (law): the name for a judge in Scotland.

Sick pay: money received by an employee who is unable to work due to illness or injury.

Signatory: someone who signs their name on an official document to register their approval of it.

Slavery: a system in which people could buy and own others (slaves) who were then made to work for no reward. (see **Forced labour**).

Solicitor: a professional person who gives legal advice and prepares documents for legal procedures, e.g. house-buying, divorce.

Speaker, the: a government official who controls the way that issues are debated in Parliament.

Stand for office: apply for election as a local councillor or MP.

Standing order: a regular payment from one bank or building society account to another (see **Direct Debit**).

Start-up loans: a sum of money given to someone to begin a new venture, and on which interest will be due later (see **Grant, interest**).

State Pension: a government payment made at regular intervals to those who have retired from work, usually at age 65 or older.

Stepfamily: a family in which one parent-figure is not the biological parent of one or more of the children.

Strike, to go on: refuse to work in order to protest against something, e.g. poor or unfair working conditions.

Subscribe to a magazine: to pay for regular postal delivery of a magazine of interest, sometimes at a substantial discount.

Successor (government): someone who takes over power, e.g. upon the death of a predecessor.

Surveyor (housing): a person who examines and checks the condition of a building prior to a sale, and then writes a survey report giving information to the house-buyer about any problems or repairs needed.

Suspect (crime): someone who police feel may be guilty of a crime.

Suspend: to officially stop something, generally for just a short time.

T

Taster session (training): a short introduction to a course to enable prospective students to try it out.

Tenancy: a rental period – often also relating to conditions about renting the property.

Tenant: a person who rents accommodation from a landlord.

Terrorism: random violence used by people who want to force change upon governments and those in authority.

Theft: the criminal act of stealing (see **Burglary**).

Therapist (psychology): a professional counsellor who tries to identify peoples' emotional problems, and works with them to find a solution.

Timescale: an anticipated period of time necessary to complete something, usually at work.

Toddler (family): a small child of between one and two years old, at a time when it's learning to walk.

Torture: to act with extreme and purposeful cruelty, e.g. to make a person give information or to punish them.

Tow away a car: use another vehicle to remove a car that is illegally parked.

Trade Union: an association of employees that work together to protect their political rights.

Trader: someone who buys and sells goods.

Treaty: an official written governmental agreement made between countries.

Tried in front of a judge: to be brought before a judge for the facts of a case to be heard, and then to be sentenced in an official court of law.

Tuition fees: money paid to a tutor or school for teaching.

U

Unemployed: not working or earning.

Uprising: a violent rebellion against an authority.

Utilities, public: public services, e.g. electricity, gas or water supplies.

V

Vacancy (employment): a job that has become available and which an employer needs to fill.

Valid: something that is legally acceptable.

Vehicle (transport): something to travel in on the roads, e.g. a car or bus.

Vetoed, to be vetoed: refused or to be denied.

Victim: someone who has been harmed by something that a person has done, or by a particular situation.

Vocational course: lessons in the practical skills necessary to a particular job, e.g. to become a plumber or a car mechanic.

Volt: a measurement of electrical force.

Voluntarily: done freely, without force or obligation.

Voluntary work: unpaid work, e.g. for a charity (see **Volunteer**).

Volunteer: someone who chooses to work without monetary payment (see **Voluntary work**).

Vulnerable people: people who are at risk of harm, either because of their age or their home/work surroundings.

W

Wages (pay): a sum of money paid to an employee.

War effort: the work that people chose to do to support the country during wartime.

Welfare benefits: money paid by the government to needy people who are unable to work, whether for reasons of illness, disability, old age or because they are caring for a sick relative.

Will (law): a legal document which is prepared in order to leave a deceased person's instructions and wishes concerning the disposal of their assets.

Withdraw (law): to step back, or to remove oneself from a formal arrangement.

Withdraw (money): remove money from a cash machine or a bank or building society.

Workforce: people who work in a particular line of business, or all who can work in a particular country or part of the world.

Working days: the usual days for work – in the UK, these are Monday, Tuesday, Wednesday, Thursday and Friday.

Y

Yellow Pages: a book that lists the details of businesses, services and organisations in an area.

APPENDIX D:
ANSWERS TO THE PRACTICE QUESTIONS

Check your answers against the correct
answers below.

Chapter Two: A Changing Society

1. B
2. False – the UK has not been invaded in the past 900 years.
3. C
4. True
5. D
6. C
7. B
8. False – they came from the countries of the former Russian Empire.
9. True
10. A
11. C
12. D
13. False
14. A
15. B & D
16. False
17. A
18. D
19. True
20. False
21. D
22. False – they didn't obtain this right until 1928.
23. True
24. B
25. B
26. True
27. B
28. False – women make up 51 per cent of the population and 45 per cent of the workforce.
29. True
30. True
31. B
32. False – girls do better at school than boys.
33. A
34. C
35. False – almost a quarter live in lone-parents families.
36. D
37. A & D
38. True
39. C
40. B
41. D
42. A & D
43. C
44. False – a third of young people go on to higher education.
45. B
46. A
47. False – under 18s cannot buy or sell alcohol.
48. C
49. True
50. D
51. False – it is, however, illegal to be drunk in a public place.
52. True

53. A & C
54. A
55. C
56. B
57. A
58. A & C
59. False – 86 per cent of young people said they **had** been involved in a community event in the preceding year.
60. C

Chapter Three: UK Today: A Profile

1. C
2. C
3. D
4. B
5. False – both the birth rate and the death rate are falling in the UK.
6. A
7. True
8. False – the first census was taken in 1801.
9. D
10. B
11. False – the information is kept confidential for 100 years.
12. A
13. B
14. C
15. True – 92 per cent of the UK's population is classed as white.
16. B
17. False – ethnic minorities make up almost one third of Great London's population.
18. B
19. C

20. False – the correct answer is John O'Groats.
21. B
22. B & D
23. True
24. A
25. B
26. False – the Scots and Northern Irish are more likely to attend a religious service than the English or Welsh.
27. D
28. C
29. False – a tenth (10%) of British Christians are Roman Catholics.
30. C
31. B & C
32. C
33. True
34. D
35. C
36. A
37. True – St Patrick's Day is a public holiday in Northern Ireland.
38. B
39. False – St George is the patron saint of England. Britain doesn't have a patron saint.
40. False – there's a major arts festival in Edinburgh each year.
41. C
42. True – all children in UK schools are taught about all religious festivals.
43. B
44. True – 2nd January is a public holiday in Scotland.
45. C
46. D
47. C

48. True – these are called April Fool's jokes.

49. A & C

50. D

51. B

52. B

53. True – they remember those who died in all wars.

54. D

55. False – Christmas celebrates the birth of Jesus Christ.

56. A

57. False – Father Christmas wears a red suit and has a long white beard.

58. A & C

59. B

60. False – England, Scotland, Wales and Northern Ireland each have a national team but there's no British team.

Chapter Four: How the United Kingdom is Governed

1. B

2. False – the British Constitution has never been written down.

3. C

4. B

5. D

6. B – the Queen cannot tell the Prime Minster what to do.

7. B

8. A

9. C

10. True

11. D

12. False – they're decided by the 'first past the post' system.

13. B

14. A

15. B

16. D

17. False – the House of Lords can propose new laws or suggest amendments to existing laws, but it cannot pass new laws; only the MPs in the Commons can do that.

18. B & D

19. A & D

20. A

21. False – the Chancellor of the Exchequer is responsible for the economy, while the Lord Chancellor is responsible for legal affairs.

22. B

23. D

24. A

25. C

26. A & D

27. A

28. C

29. True – civil servants must remain politically neutral.

30. A

31. D

32. A

33. D – there is no devolved administration for England.

34. B

35. B

36. C & D

37. False – council tax applies to every domestic dwelling, including mobile homes and house boats.

38. B

39. C

40. B

41. False – the police have 'operational independence', which means that the

government cannot tell them what to do in any particular case.

42. A

43. C

44. A

45. A

46. False – EU citizens who are resident in the UK can vote in   some elections, but they cannot vote in national parliamentary (general) elections.

47. D

48. A

49. B

50. B

51. A

52. C

53. False – the European Union was founded in 1957 but the UK didn't join until 1973.

54. D

55. A & D

56. A & C

57. D

58. False – there are European directives about making people redundant as well as regulations limiting the amount of hours people can be made to work.

59. C

60. A

Chapter Five: Everyday Needs

1. B

2. D

3. B

4. False – in Scotland, the seller sets a price for their property and potential buyers make offers over that amount.

5. A

6. B

7. A

8. B

9. False – if there is damage to the property, the landlord will keep the deposit to cover any costs.

10. D

11. A

12. B & C

13. C

14. True

15. B

16. C

17. B & C

18. B

19. D

20. False – but if you have a mortgage, the lender will insist on you having buildings insurance to safeguard the property.

21. C

22. A & D

23. B

24. False – the credit card company pays for the purchase and sends you a bill.

25. D

26. A

27. B

28. C

29. B

30. B & C

31. True

32. B

33. C

34. B

35. A & C

36. D

37. B – except for Northern Ireland,

where children must start school at the age of four.

38. A – most areas have two stages, known as primary and secondary education, but in a few places there are three stages, which are called primary, middle and senior school.

39. C

40. True

41. B

42. B

43. A

44. C

45. True

46. C

47. A

48. C – 'PG' stands for parental guidance.

49. False – only adults aged 18 or over can watch an 18 rated film.

50. A

51. D

52. C

53. False – not cleaning up after your dog in a public place is an offence and you may receive a penalty fine.

54. B

55. D

56. D

57. B

58. False – Sikh men wear a turban as part of their religion, so they don't have to wear a crash helmet, but everyone else does.

59. C – but if someone is injured you must call the police and an ambulance.

60. B

Chapter Six: Employment

1. B

2. C

3. A

4. D

5. B & C

6. True

7. A

8. A

9. B & C

10. C

11. D

12. False – a person's weight and personal hygiene are not covered by discrimination laws.

13. B

14. True – this is an additional law which only applies in Northern Ireland.

15. D

16. A & D

17. B – the laws on sexual harassment apply to both sexes.

18. A

19. B

20. A & C

21. C

22. B

23. C

24. B

25. C & D

26. False – not everyone needs to fill in a tax return, but everyone who works in the UK must pay income tax.

27. B

28. D

29. B

30. C

31. A

32. C & D
33. D
34. D
35. False – men are eligible at 65 and women are eligible at 60, but the retirement age for women is changing and by 2020, the retirement age for both sexes will be 65.
36. A & C
37. C
38. D
39. B
40. B & D
41. B
42. B & C
43. True – Employment Tribunals make decisions on cases of unfair dismissal.
44. C
45. B
46. A
47. A
48. False – self-employed people pay their income tax once a year.
49. B
50. C
51. B
52. A
53. C
54. D
55. C
56. True
57. B
58. D
59. A
60. B & D

Llangollen, Clwyd, Wales

INDEX

Survival Books

S urvival Books was established in 1987 and by the mid-'90s was the leading publisher of books for people planning to live, work, buy property or retire abroad.

From the outset, our philosophy has been to provide the most comprehensive and up-to-date information available. Our titles routinely contain up to twice as much information as other books and are updated frequently. All our books contain colour photographs and some are printed in two colours or full colour throughout. They also contain original cartoons, illustrations and maps.

Survival Books are written by people with first-hand experience of the countries and the people they describe, and therefore provide invaluable insights that cannot be obtained from official publications or websites, and information that is more reliable and objective than that provided by the majority of unofficial sites.

Survival Books are designed to be easy – and interesting – to read. They contain a comprehensive list of contents and index and extensive appendices, including useful addresses, further reading, useful websites and glossaries to help you obtain additional information as well as metric conversion tables and other useful reference material.

Our primary goal is to provide you with the essential information necessary for a trouble-free life or property purchase and to save you time, trouble and money.

We believe our books are the best – they are certainly the best-selling. But don't take our word for it – read what reviewers and readers have said about Survival Books at the front of this book.

Order your copies today by phone, fax, post or email from:
Survival Books, PO Box 3780, Yeovil, BA21 5WX, United Kingdom.
Tel: +44 (0)1935-700060, email: sales@survivalbooks.net,
Website: www.survivalbooks.net

Buying a Home Series

Buying a home abroad is not only a major financial transaction but also a potentially life-changing experience; it's therefore essential to get it right. Our Buying a Home guides are required reading for anyone planning to purchase property abroad and are packed with vital information to guide you through the property jungle and help you avoid disasters that can turn a dream home into a nightmare.

The purpose of our Buying a Home guides is to enable you to choose the most favourable location and the most appropriate property for your requirements, and to reduce your risk of making an expensive mistake by making informed decisions and calculated judgements rather than uneducated and hopeful guesses. Most importantly, they will help you save money and will repay your investment many times over.

Buying a Home guides are the most comprehensive and up-to-date source of information available about buying property abroad – whether you're seeking a detached house or an apartment, a holiday or a permanent home (or an investment property), these books will prove invaluable.

For a full list of our current titles, visit our website at www.survivalbooks.net

Living and Working Series

Our Living and Working guides are essential reading for anyone planning to spend a period abroad – whether it's an extended holiday or permanent migration – and are packed with priceless information designed to help you avoid costly mistakes and save both time and money.

Living and Working guides are the most comprehensive and up-to-date source of practical information available about everyday life abroad. They aren't, however, simply a catalogue of dry facts and figures, but are written in a highly readable style – entertaining, practical and occasionally humorous.

Our aim is to provide you with the comprehensive practical information necessary for a trouble-free life. You may have visited a country as a tourist, but living and working there is a different matter altogether; adjusting to a new environment and culture and making a home in any foreign country can be a traumatic and stressful experience. You need to adapt to new customs and traditions, discover the local way of doing things (such as finding a home, paying bills and obtaining insurance) and learn all over again how to overcome the everyday obstacles of life.

All these subjects and many, many more are covered in depth in our Living and Working guides – don't leave home without them.

The Expats' Best Friend!

Culture Wise Series

O ur **Culture Wise** series of guides is essential reading for anyone who wants to understand how a country really 'works'. Whether you're planning to stay for a few days or a lifetime, these guides will help you quickly find your feet and settle into your new surroundings.

Culture Wise guides:

- Reduce the anxiety factor in adapting to a foreign culture
- Explain how to behave in everyday situations in order to avoid cultural and social gaffes
- Help you get along with your neighbours
- Make friends and establish lasting business relationships
- Enhance your understanding of a country and its people.

People often underestimate the extent of cultural isolation they can face abroad, particularly in a country with a different language. At first glance, many countries seem an 'easy' option, often with millions of visitors from all corners of the globe and well-established expatriate communities. But, sooner or later, newcomers find that most countries are indeed 'foreign' and many come unstuck as a result. **Culture Wise** guides will enable you to quickly adapt to the local way of life and feel at home, and – just as importantly – avoid the worst effects of culture shock.

Culture Wise – The Wise Way to Travel

The essential guides to Culture, Customs & Business Etiquette

Other Survival Books

The Best Places to Buy a Home in France/Spain: Unique guides to where to buy property in Spain and France, containing detailed regional profiles and market reports.

Buying, Selling and Letting Property: The best source of information about buying, selling and letting property in the UK.

Earning Money From Your French Home: Income from property in France, including short- and long-term letting.

Investing in Property Abroad: Everything you need to know and more about buying property abroad for investment and pleasure.

Making a Living: Comprehensive guides to self-employment and starting a business in France and Spain.

Renovating & Maintaining Your French Home: The ultimate guide to renovating and maintaining your dream home in France.

Retiring in France/Spain: Everything a prospective retiree needs to know about the two most popular international retirement destinations.

Running Gîtes and B&Bs in France: An essential book for anyone planning to invest in a gîte or bed & breakfast business.

Rural Living in France: An invaluable book for anyone seeking the 'good life', containing a wealth of practical information about all aspects of French country life.

Shooting Caterpillars in Spain: The hilarious and compelling story of two innocents abroad in the depths of Andalusia in the late '80s.

For a full list of our current titles, visit our website at www.survivalbooks.net

LIVING & WORKING IN
BRITAIN

What's it really like Living and Working in Britain? Not surprisingly, there's a lot more to life than castles, cricket and crumpets. This book is guaranteed to make your life in Britain easier and more enjoyable. Regardless of whether you're planning to stay for a few weeks or indefinitely, *Living and Working in Britain* has been written for you.

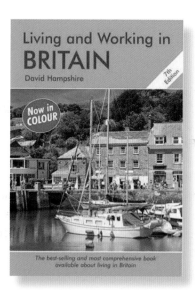

PRINTED IN COLOUR!

Topics include:

- ◆ How to find a job with a good salary and conditions
- ◆ How to obtain a residence or work permit
- ◆ How to avoid and overcome problems on arrival
- ◆ How to find your dream home
- ◆ How to make the most of post office and telephone services
- ◆ How to get the best education for your family
- ◆ How to make the best use of public transport and much, much more.

Living and Working in Britain is the most comprehensive and up-to-date source of practical information available about everyday life in Britain. It's packed with 400 pages of important and useful data, designed to help you avoid costly mistakes and save both time and money.

Buy your copy today at www.survivalbooks.net

Survival Books – The Expatriates' Best Friend

CULTURE WISE ENGLAND

The Essential Guide to Culture, Customs & Business Etiquette

Travellers often underestimate the depth of cultural isolation they can face abroad, even in a country where English is spoken. *Culture Wise England* will help you understand England and its people and adapt to the English way of life. Most importantly, it will enable you to quickly feel at home.

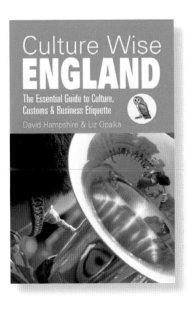

PRINTED IN COLOUR!

Topics include:

- ◆ How to overcome culture shock
- ◆ The historical and political background to modern England
- ◆ English attitudes and values – at home and at work
- ◆ Do's, don'ts and taboos
- ◆ How to enjoy yourself in English style
- ◆ Business and professional etiquette
- ◆ England's spoken and body language
- ◆ Getting around England safely
- ◆ Shopping the English way

Culture Wise England is essential reading for visitors and residents who want to understand how the country really works. Whether you're planning to stay for a few weeks or a lifetime, it will quickly help you find you feet after arrival, settle in smoothly and integrate into your new surroundings.

Buy your copy today at www.survivalbooks.net

Survival Books – The Wisest Way to Travel

LIVING & WORKING IN
LONDON

What's it really like living and working in London? Not surprisingly there's a lot more to life than bobbies, beefeaters and busbys! This book is guaranteed to hasten your introduction to the London way of life and, most importantly, it will save you time, trouble and money. Regardless of whether you're planning to stay for a few weeks or indefinitely, *Living and Working in London* has been written for you!

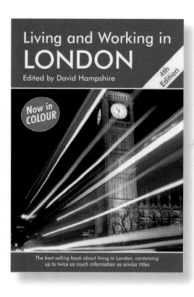

PRINTED IN COLOUR!

Topics include:

♦ How to find a job with a good salary and conditions

♦ How to avoid and overcome problems on arrival

♦ How to find somewhere to live

♦ How to find the best schools

♦ How to obtain the best health treatment

♦ How to stretch your pounds further

♦ How to make the best use of public transport and much, much more.

Living and Working in London is the most comprehensive source of practical information available about everyday life in London. It's packed with over 350 pages of important and useful data, designed to help you avoid costly mistakes and save both time and money.

Buy your copy today at www.survivalbooks.net

Survival Books – The Expatriates' Best Friend

BUYING, SELLING & LETTING PROPERTY

Buying, Selling & Letting Property is essential reading for anyone who owns or is planning to buy a home in the UK, and is designed to guide you through the property maze and save you time trouble and money! Most importantly it is packed with vital information to help you avoid disasters that can turn your dream home into a nightmare!

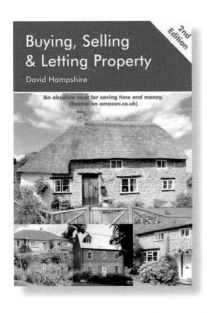

Buying, Selling
& Letting Property

David Hampshire

'An absolute must for saving time and money.'
(Reader on amazon.co.uk)

2nd Edition

Topics include:

- ◆ Choosing the location
- ◆ What to buy
- ◆ The buying process
- ◆ Mortgages
- ◆ Moving house
- ◆ Home improvements
- ◆ Letting
- ◆ Selling your home
- ◆ Useful addresses, publications & websites
- ◆ Comprehensive glossary, checklists and much, much more.

Buying, Selling & Letting Property is the most comprehensive book about buying property in the UK.

Buy your copy today at www.survivalbooks.net

Survival Books – The Homebuyers' Friend

PHOTO

CREDITS

www.shutterstock.com

pages 19 © Lawrence Beck, 32 © Diego Cervo, 32 © HomeStudio, 89 © Gordon Swanson, 126 © EML, 131 © EML, 149 © EML, 161 © Alexander Gitlits, 161 © Ian Edward Schofield, 172 © Mark Yuill, 222 © Dmitry Pichugin, 223 © Yury Zaporozhchenko, 223 © Colin & Linda McKie

Peter Farmer

© pages 19, 45, 67

www.britainonview.com

© pages 10, 46, 77, 178, 208

Bamburgh Castle, Northumberland